The Red Baron

The Red Baron

A History in Pictures

Norman Franks

Pen & Sword
AVIATION

First published in Great Britain in 2016 by
Pen & Sword Aviation
an imprint of
Pen & Sword Books Ltd,
47 Church Street, Barnsley,
South Yorkshire.
S70 2AS

ISBN 978-1-47386-122-0

A CIP catalogue record for this book is available
from the British Library

Typeset in Ehrhardt by Mac Style Ltd, Bridlington, East Yorkshire
Printed and bound in Great Britain by CPI

Pen & Sword Books Ltd incorporates the imprints of
Pen & Sword Aviation, Pen & Sword Family History, Pen & Sword Maritime,
Pen & Sword Military, Pen & Sword Discovery, Wharncliffe Local History,
Wharncliffe True Crime, Wharncliffe Transport, Pen and Sword Select,
Pen and Sword Military Classics

For a complete list of Pen & Sword titles please contact:
Pen & Sword Books limited
47 Church Street, Barnsley, South Yorkshire, S70 2AS, England.
E-mail: enquiries@pen-and-sword.co.uk
Website: www.pen-and-sword.co.uk

Contents

Chapter One

From Soldier to Airman

There can be few people who have not heard of the name of Manfred von Richthofen, or perhaps the more usual term 'The Red Baron' (although he never was a 'baron', that title being held by his father). He was born into a world so different from modern times that few of us would recognise Europe as it was then, not understanding that for the majority of upper-class Germans military service was a duty, and not something that had to be endured for a short time similar to national service. So it would have been perfectly natural for him and his brother Lothar to become soldiers for the Fatherland without a second thought.

Freiherr Manfred Albrecht von Richthofen, the eldest son of *Rittmeister* Albrecht Philipp Karl Julius von Richthofen, serving with the *Leibkürassier* Regiment, was born on 2 May 1892, a brother for sister Ilse, born in 1890. Albrecht was thirty-three years of age when Manfred was born, and he had married Kunigarde von Schickfus und Neudorff, from a wealthy Silesian family. Kunigarde's father Leopold inherited his father's estates, while also marrying Therese, the daughter of Baron von Falkenhausen of Wallisfurth. Thus the family itself was wealthy, with a place in society, not that Albrecht and his bride saw much of it, he having to rely mostly on his army pay. Indeed, when their children came along they were living in an apartment in Kleinburg, in the suburbs of Breslau (now part of the city of Wrocław, Poland).

In an endeavour to find cheaper accommodation, the family moved to Schweidnitz (now Świdnica, Poland) and, although helped by Kunigarde's allowance, when the time came for the children to begin school, there had to be a move back to Breslau, especially as brother Lothar Siegfried von Richthofen came along in September 1894. Then, plunging into an icy river to save the life of one of his soldiers, Albrecht suffered a chill that brought on a serious illness which caused deafness and he had to resign his career.

The children were schooled at home initially, but Manfred was eventually enrolled in a local grammar school before, inevitably, joining the army cadet corps. From here he was eventually assigned to the 1st *Uhlan* Cavalry Regiment in 1911. Lothar finished his schooling and joined the army in 1914, serving with the 4th Dragoon Regiment. Albrecht volunteered for limited military service with the rank of major.

This story must now jump in time. Manfred saw active duty with his regiment in the opening months of the war but, with the coming of trench warfare, cavalry units on both sides lost their traditional role of reconnaissance and stirring charges, so that many Cavalrymen turned to a more active form of duty, that of flight. Aviation was still new but it was becoming obvious that flying was going to be a major feature in a new kind of warfare, for they could fly high across the trench lines to reconnoitre for the generals and fight the opposing airmen whenever they met. It was going to be an exciting, if dangerous, occupation.

Manfred first saw cavalry duty in Russia before moving to France but was soon the recipient of the Iron Cross 2nd Class. In May 1915 he was accepted into aviation and trained to become an observer. This was quite normal in the First World War; officers were generally the 'captains' of the aeroplane, the pilot merely the driver and, more often than not, an NCO. Manfred's first operational assignment was again on the Russian front, being posted to *Flieger-Abteilung Nr. 69* (*FA.69*) but he then returned to the Western Front, joining a unit with the cover name of Mail Carrier Pigeon Unit, at Ostende, that was in reality a long-range bombing unit. It was known as BAO

(*Brieftauben-Abteilung-Ostende* (or Mail Pigeon Unit), the unit 'camouflaged' by this name.

By this time he had decided it would be preferable to fly aeroplanes rather than be a passenger and so applied for pilot training, which he completed at Döberitz; in March 1916 he was assigned to *KG.2* (*Kampfgeschwader Nr. 2*), on the Verdun (French) Front. This was at a period that saw the introduction of serious air battles between the airmen of both sides. While airmen had been happy enough firing pistols or carbines at each other if they met in the air, each side's aggressive aviators were experimenting with machine guns. The Germans had developed their Fokker *Eindecker* single-seat aeroplanes, which they assigned piecemeal among the two-seater units for escort duty, but the pilots who volunteered to fly them, once they had been fitted with a machine gun that fired through the arc of the propeller, were more than anxious to become fighter pilots and engage the Allied aeroplanes. The early aeroplanes, fitted with a propeller in the front, made it impossible to fire directly forwards, but Fokker's team invented a way of doing so, making his, until then, fairly unimpressive monoplane, a deadly aggressor in the air. The Allies, and particularly the British, took on an aggressive stance from the start, and were only too anxious to engage their opposite numbers in air battles. The age of the fighter pilot, the dogfights, the 'aces', had begun.

These early aces became household names: Max Immelmann, Oswald Boelcke, Max Mülzer, Kurt Wintgens, Otto Parschau, Hans Buddecke, Walter Höhndorf, *et a*l. They found success flying Anthony Fokker's monoplane but, because the Germans did not want the secret of their interrupter gear to be discovered, and since there were so few *eindeckers,* the fighting pilots were forbidden to cross the lines into Allied territory. From this time the Germans continued their air war in a mostly defensive mode.

By the time Manfred began looking towards becoming one of these new air heroes, several had fallen in combat, although all had achieved enough success to receive Germany's highest award for bravery, the *Orden Pour le Mérite,* a decorative gold and blue enamel cross worn at the neck; due to its blue enamelling, it was referred to as *The Blue Max.* This seemed to be a magical magnet for successive German air fighters. The first two awarded went to Max Immelmann and Oswald Boelcke; when the former was killed, Boelcke was taken away from front-line action. However, he took the time to suggest that rather than distributing Fokkers piecemeal among the two-seater units they should be gathered together in small groups to act independently. They could continue to protect their two-seater comrades while also operating aggressively against British and French aeroplanes over the front.

By the time of the Somme battles in summer 1916 Boelcke's plan had been approved and the first fighting units were beginning to form. Called *Jagdstaffeln,* hunting units, which became abbreviated to *Jastas,* the first were set up in August and September 1916, Boelcke being allowed back into combat commanding *Jasta 2.* To some degree he was allowed to handpick his pilots, and the first four were *Leutnants* Wolfgang Günther, Otto Höhne, Ernst Diener and Winard Grafe. On 1 September three more arrived, Manfred von Richthofen, and two NCO pilots, *Feldwebel* (sergeant) Leopold Reimann and *Offizierstellvertreter* (warrant officer) Max Müller, while another pilot also named Reimann, *Leutnant* Hans Reimann, quickly followed. All had some experience for it was normal for single-seat pilots to have had experience on two-seater units. This was a good way of introducing pilots to air actions, and gave them a chance to begin to understand and 'see' things in the air. As the war continued, it was more or less a requirement that those posted to a *Jasta* had to be experienced men who had flown on front-line operations and then attended a *Jastaschule.*

While still on the Russian Front, Boelcke had been interviewing potential pilots for his new unit and von Richthofen, hearing of this, made sure he was available to meet the great man. They had already met briefly, and by chance, on a train journey in France. Obviously Boelcke saw something in the young Prussian and agreed he would arrange for him to join *Jasta 2* when it was formed.

As the new unit came into being there was only one major problem: they had no aeroplanes. Eventually one turned up, a Fokker D.III biplane that Boelcke naturally made his own. Gradually, however, more aircraft began to arrive, by which time Boelcke had added to his previous score of eighteen victories by at least ten. Everyone in the *Jasta* was eager to get into action and when they did receive adequate aircraft, Fokker Ds and Albatros D.IIs, they began to fly patrols in small formations and to shoot down enemy aeroplanes.

Manfred's first kill came on the morning of 17 September, a two-seat pusher-type aircraft, an FE.2b. It crashed at Villers Plouich, and the victorious von Richthofen landed his Albatros nearby so as to inspect his handiwork. The observer had been killed in the air and the pilot mortally wounded: he died under Manfred's gaze, no doubt the first enemy he had seen do so close up. While a sobering scene, it only increased Manfred's keen sense of loyal duty to conquer more of his country's enemies.

During autumn 1916, Manfred von Richthofen gained further successes in air combat and by 4 January 1917 he had achieved sixteen victories. The early air aces had received their Blue Max decorations (*Pour le Mérite*) after eight kills, but this began to appear too easy a score to reach, and so the High Command had increased this to sixteen. Thirteen early aces, mostly Fokker pilots, had received this decoration by the end of 1916, all under the lower kill criteria. Richthofen was the fourteenth, and the first for the new year. His was awarded on 14 January 1917. Another feature of awards to German soldiers was that they came thick and fast once they started. To be eligible for the Blue

Max one generally had to have been awarded one or both classes of the Iron Cross, and an immediate prerequisite was the award of the Royal House of Hohenzollern Order. As Germany was a federation of a number of states, such as Prussia, Saxony, Württemburg, Bavaria, etc., once one state awarded someone a high decoration, others felt obliged to award their state's decorations to the man too. It must have been heady stuff for these young men to be in receipt of such colourful medals, crosses and orders, with the accompanying adulation.

By this time, however, von Richthofen's great mentor, Boelcke, had been killed following a mid-air collision in October. He had achieved a remarkable, for the period, forty victories in air combat. Virtually all of his contemporaries had fallen by this time, and for the next fifteen months, from January 1917 to March 1918, Manfred would be the German top scorer each month.

Richthofen had begun to make a name for himself, not least by shooting down one of Britain's early air heroes, Major Lanoe Hawker VC DSO, in a duel on 23 November. Hawker had been flying a single-seat DH.2 pusher fighter. Two more DH2s followed in December, one being flown by another early RFC ace, Lieutenant A. G. Knight DSO MC on the 20th.

Another he 'claimed' was flown by a future air hero, Sergeant J. T. B. McCudden. McCudden was flying his DH.2 on 27 December and, for once, Richthofen chased it across the British lines and saw it go spinning down to what he thought would be an inevitable crash. However, McCudden eased out of the spin and later flew home. To try to have this kill confirmed, Richthofen's adjutant would have telephoned to the German front-line trenches to see if someone had witnessed a *gitterrumpf* fall into Allied lines. The German word *gitterrumpf* meant 'lattice tail', i.e. an aeroplane with twin booms rather than a fuselage. They may well have confirmed seeing such an aircraft go down, but obviously, in this case, could not have confirmed its actual demise. Later historians tried to speculate that it must have been an FE.2b pusher but, although one was forced to land on the British side, the time of the combat was nowhere close to Richthofen's action. Another FE.2b to be forced down this day was flown by Lieutenant D. C. Cunnell of 20 Squadron, but this was too far to the north. Cunnell had nothing at all to do with Richthofen, although these two would meet later.

By sheer good fortune I met Sue Fischer in Toronto in 1996, and she helped me with research by going through Floyd Gibbons' notes at Maine University. Among several seemingly interesting letters she copied and sent to me was reference to McCudden as an NCO. It was only when wondering why Gibbons would ask the Air Ministry in London about him that two and two were gradually added together.

Because the McCudden action was never contemplated during earlier historians' research into Manfred's combat claims, I will record here the combat reports of Manfred, McCudden, and two other pilots in the 29 Squadron patrol. First is a list of 29's six pilots on this patrol, who took off from their base at le Hameau, at 1350 hours:

Name	DH2	Time down
Captain H. J. Payn	7849	1535
Lieutenant Dickson	A2591	landed at la Bellevue
Lieutenant C. H. B. Readman	7855	1430 – plug trouble
Flight Sergeant J. T. B. McCudden	5985	1615
Lieutenant A. Jennings	5957	1615
Lieutenant G. R. T. Hill	7939	1520 – engine trouble

Richthofen's report:

> *1625 hrs. above Ficheux, south of Arras.*
> *FE two-seater was smashed, number etc. not recognisable.*

> *At 1615, five planes of our staffel attacked enemy squadron south of*
> *Arras. The enemy approached our lines, but was turned back. After*
> *some fighting I managed to attack a very courageously flown Vickers*
> *two-seater. After 300 shots, enemy plane began dropping uncontrolled.*
> *I pursued the plane up to 1,000 metres above the ground on enemy side,*
> *one kilometre behind trenches near Ficheux.*

(Although the Baron records his opponent as a two-seater FE, the only FE casualties this day were a machine from 11 Squadron – but the combat took place at 1115 hours – and, as already mentioned, a 20 Squadron machine, hit by ground-fire, coming down near Berthen, west of the lines, and burnt by the crew. Berthen is inland from Calais, so too far north, and the Squadron were based at Clairmarais. I believe the British translation of Manfred's report was coloured by the belief that the '*gitterrumpf*' referred to had to be an FE rather than a DH.2.)

Captain Payn's report:

> *At about 2.40 pm, whilst on Offensive Patrol flying between Neuville*
> *Vitasse and Ayette, at 8,500 ft I saw two machines flying close together*
> *over Boiry St Rictrude. I dived on them firing and the rest of the*
> *patrol followed. Both H.A.* [Hostile Aircraft] *were driven down, one*
> *appeared to be out of control, but was lost sight of before reaching the*
> *ground. They did not appear again in the locality of our patrol.*
> *   Later (about 3 pm) six Albatros Scouts were patrolling at 12,000*
> *ft to the East of us. Our A.A. batteries fired many indicating rounds.*

The patrol was then three De Havillands and two Nieuports. I fired several rounds up at the H.A. scouts hoping to get them down to our level, then being about 11,000 ft.

About 3 pm I saw a Walfish scout flying S. below at 9,000 ft. I dived firing several rounds at about 150 yds range.

When again at 10,500 ft the H.A. which kept splendid formation dived onto the nearest De Havilland. One H.A. would leave the formation and attack, expending a few rounds in diving. Finally the six Scouts attacked and many rounds were fired under 50 yds range. I observed only three De Havillands and one Nieuport in this attack. One De Havilland went down in a left hand spin with the H.A. Scout following. I dived after the latter and fired my remaining shots into him whereupon he left the De Havilland.

Having no further ammunition and unable to use the main tank, I fired a green light [signal flare] *and came home.*

Second Lieutenant A. Jennings' report:

Six H.A. patrolling up and down the lines parallel to us and gradually approaching nearer. About 3 pm they began making dives at us firing at long range. I fired a few rounds in return, then one of our machines turned while we were over Adinfer Wood and went South. The rest of the patrol followed. Two H.A. dived at the leading De Havilland. I dived on one of the H.A. and got off some 20 rounds. While doing this another H.A. appeared from half right. I turned towards it and fired at very short range. I could plainly see the pilot, then two H.A. got on my tail and another De Havilland drove them off. My engine cut out and, thinking the petrol pipe cut, I made for the lines. In a minute or so my engine came on again. I turned round and saw one De Havilland apparently in a spin with an H.A. in pursuit. I went down and the H.A. went off. The De Havilland regained control and two Nieuports then appeared and the H.A. drew off.

McCudden's report:

> *Going east of Adinfer I saw five H.A. Lt Jennings attacked a H.A.*
> *and another H.A. was approaching from behind. I fired about 15 shots*
> *and drove him off. He turned and came towards me, firing. I opened*
> *fire at 100 yds and after about eight shots my gun stopped, due to a*
> *cross-feed. As the hostile machine was engaging me at close range, I*
> *turned on my back and dived vertically, in a slow spin and in this way*
> *regained our lines. At 800 ft, over Passeux the H.A. left me.*
>
> *I quickly rectified the stoppage and followed the H.A. across the*
> *trenches at 2,000 ft. Owing to his superior speed and climb he out-*
> *distanced me and rejoined his patrol at about 5,000 ft. The hostile*
> *patrol then withdrew.*

It would seem that McCudden had driven off von Richthofen's attack
on Jennings and, shortly afterwards, Jennings saw McCudden spinning
earthwards, being followed by the Baron. No doubt the latter, realising
he was near the front lines, quickly decided to head back into German-
held territory, and probably was not aware that McCudden, having
pulled out of his spin, was attempting to follow. It would also seem
that von Richthofen, believing his opponent was just moments away
from smashing into the ground, brought this wishful thinking into his
combat report. Once the *Jasta* had telephoned the front-line observers
to ask if they had seen a *gitterrumpf* going down in a spin, and they
reported that they had, the 'confirmation' was complete. Had they
also reported that the enemy machine was a DH.2, von Richthofen's
report would have recorded this rather than an FE.2, i.e. a single-seater
rather than a two-seater. There is, of course, no answer to him saying
that the machine was smashed and therefore the serial number was
unrecognisable. As it would have 'fallen' inside British lines, he would
not know how unrecognisable it was.

In his book *Flying Fury*, McCudden states:

I now fired at the nearest Hun who was after Jennings, and this Hun at once came for me nose on, and we both fired simultaneously, but after firing about twenty shots my gun got a bad double feed, which I could not rectify at the time as I was now in the middle of five D.I Albatroses, so I half-rolled. When coming out I kept the machine past vertical for a few hundred feet and had started to level out again, when, 'cack, cack, cack, cack', came from just behind me. I immediately half-rolled again, but still the Hun stayed there, and so whilst half-rolling, I kept on making headway for our lines, for the fight had started east of Adinfer Wood, with which we were so familiar on our previous little joy-jaunts.

I continued to do half-rolls and got over the trenches at about 2,000 feet, with the Hun still in pursuit, and the rascal drove me down to 800 feet a mile west of the lines, when he turned off east, and was shelled by our A.A. guns. I soon rectified the jam and turned to chase the Hun, but by this time the Hun was much higher, and very soon joined his patrol, who were waiting for him at about 5,000 feet over Rancourt.

An interesting fact is that the 29 Squadron flight commander, Herbert Payn, had, in 1915, flown with Lanoe Hawker as his observer/gunner in No. 6 Squadron, flying FE.2a machines. Had things been different, Payn might well have avenged the death of his former pilot on this December afternoon. In February 1917 Payn was lucky to survive an encounter with Werner Voss.

* * *

Things were now going to change for Manfred. With sixteen victories and the Blue Max at his throat, he was given command of his own *Jasta* on 6 January 1917. *Jasta 11* had become operational in October 1916, under *Oberleutnant* Emil Lang, and was based at Douai on the German Sixth Army Front. It had achieved no victories since its formation, and it would be Manfred who would score its first, an FE.8 single-seat pusher scout, on 23 January. In fact he would claim the *Jasta*'s first three, but the unit would gain undying fame under his leadership and be one of the most successful fighter units of the German Air Service (*Luftskreitkräfte*).

Leutnant Georg Zeumer was Manfred von Richthofen's pilot on the Russian Front whilst serving with *FA.69* on Albatros C two-seaters. On returning to France to serve with *BAO*, Zeumer came too, probably flying the large AEG G.II aeroplanes. These were twin-engined, the propellers of which were perilously close to Manfred's front cockpit. Zeumer later flew with *Jasta 2* in 1917 by which time he was suffering from tuberculosis. He was killed in action on 17 June, a quicker end to his suffering.

An Albatros C two-seater reconnaissance machine, the type used by Zeumer and von Richthofen on the Russian Front in 1916.

Oswald Boelcke, Manfred's mentor, who selected him to join *Jasta 2* in summer 1916. At his throat is the *Pour le Mérite*. Through the first button-hole is the ribbon and swords of the Hohenzollern Order and the ribbon of the Iron Cross 2nd Class. The Iron Cross 1st Class is on the right, above the pilot's flying badge.

Jasta 2 soon after it received its aeroplanes, the Albatros D.II single-seat fighter. These are drawn up on the flying field at Lagnicourt, France, where the *Jasta* began operations in September 1916.

2/Lt L. B. F. Morris, No. 11 Squadron RFC, and 3rd Royal West Surrey Regiment. Lionel Morris was the pilot of Manfred's first combat victory on 17 September 1916. Manfred landed near to the crash although he died shortly afterwards. He was nineteen years old.

Captain Tom Rees, formerly with the 14th Royal Welsh Fusiliers, was Morris's observer. He was twenty-one years of age and was killed in the air during the fight. Tom's brother John was killed in November 1916 while cutting down a tree with his father, when the tree fell on him. His parents believed Tom might well be a prisoner but news arrived confirming his death on the morning of John's funeral. This information is updated from *Under the Guns of the Red Baron* by Franks, Giblin and McCrery (Grub Street, 1995).

The FE.2b, a pusher-type, the engine being behind the crew's gondola, pushing the aeroplane forward; it gave the observer a good arc of fire from the front cockpit. Morris and Rees were flying such a machine when Manfred brought them down near Villers-Plouich, near Gonnelieu.

The *Ehrenbecher* victory cup was presented to an airman of whatever capacity, when credited with his first combat victory. Richthofen would have received one following the fight on 17 September 1916, and it came with a victory certificate. Richthofen decided he would like an additional memorial and, in anticipation of further victories, ordered a small silver cup from a Berlin jeweller, which was engraved with the date and type of victory. As is well known, later in the war silver became scarce in Germany and after producing sixty such victory cups, von Richthofen did not want to continue using a base metal. Towards the end of the Second World War, when Richthofen's former home was overrun by Russian forces, much of his memorabilia was lost, including the cups.

Further victories included 2/Lt W. C. Fenwick's BE.12 (21 Sqn) on 7 October, falling near Equancourt on 7 October. William Fenwick, from London, was nineteen years old, and has no known grave. In *Under the Guns of the Red Baron* we state he was an only son, but it is now known that he had one brother and two sisters.

Oswald Boelcke returning from patrol in his Albatros D.II at Lagnicourt. Manfred stands on the extreme left, with Stefan Kirmaier on his right. The man with the white band round his cap is Erich König. Richthofen stands to König's left with his back to the camera.

Stefan Kirmaier shot down this BE.2c of 12 Squadron on 21 October; the pilot, 2/Lt A. B. Raymond-Barker became a prisoner of war. It was the German's sixth victory. In April 1918, Manfred von Richthofen would shoot down Raymond-Barker's brother.

The remains of a 12 Squadron BE.2c (2506), Manfred's eighth victory, scored on 9 November 1916; 2/Lt I. G. Cameron died in this action.

Oswald Boelcke standing in front of his Albatros Scout (D386), suited up ready for flight. His machine had no special markings but note the leader's identifying streamer attached to the trailing edge of the lower wing, which would be repeated on the other side. Boelcke was killed in this machine on 28 October, in a mid-air collision.

Friend and fellow airman to Boelcke, Erwin Böhme of *Jasta 2* had the great misfortune to be the pilot who collided with him, during a fight with DH.2s of 24 Squadron. Böhme survived the collision and went on to shoot down twenty-four Allied aircraft and win the Blue Max before falling in combat on 29 November. By one of those strange quirks of fate, his brother Martin was killed on 21 April 1918 during a bombing raid on St Omer, the same day von Richthofen met his end.

Oberleutnant Stefan Kirmaier took command of *Jasta 2* following Boelcke's loss. By special decree the *Jasta* then became known as *Jasta* Boelcke. He had earlier been a Fokker pilot with *Kek* Jametz, which whom he scored three victories. He had brought his score to eleven by 22 November, the day he too fell in combat, with the DH.2s of 24 Squadron RFC.

Kirmaier (left) with Hans Imelmann, a grinning von Richthofen and Hans Wortmann, in front of an Albatros D.II. Imelmann (note spelling) is no relation to Max Immelmann. The reason for the binoculars was so that pilots could train them on the front line, watching from their airfield for the approach of Allied aircraft, whereupon they would take to the air. Imelmann was killed on 23 January 1917, Wortmann on 2 April.

Jasta 2's Albatros Scouts prepare for flight at Lagnicourt. Richthofen in his light-coloured pullover is training his field-glasses on the distant front line. Imelmann and Kirmaier stand close by.

Jasta 2 shortly before Kirmaier's demise. L to R: Jürgan Sandel, Max Müller, von Richthofen, Wolfgang Günther, Kirmaier, Hans Imelmann, Erich König, Otto Walter Höhne, Hans Wortmann and Dieter Collin. Müller would become a leading ace before his death in January 1918, and Collin would later command *Jasta* 56.

The de Havilland 2 single-seat pusher fighter. The pilot had a good field of fire forwards, as the propeller in all pusher types was behind. Lanoe Hawker, A. G. Knight and James McCudden all had fights with von Richthofen in such an aeroplane in the winter of 1916.

Major Lanoe Hawker VC DSO was a month short of his twenty-sixth birthday when he met von Richthofen in combat on 23 November. Following a prolonged dogfight, Hawker had finally to attempt to race for the lines before his petrol became exhausted, and paid with his life.

Another successful air fighter was Captain A. G. Knight DSO MC, of 29 Squadron. Although English by birth, he had spent his early years in Canada. On 20 December 1916 he was all set for Christmas leave but met von Richthofen in combat above Monchy. Following some keen sparing, von Richthofen's fire appeared to hit Arthur Knight and his DH.2 fell to earth in a series of curves before it was dashed to pieces.

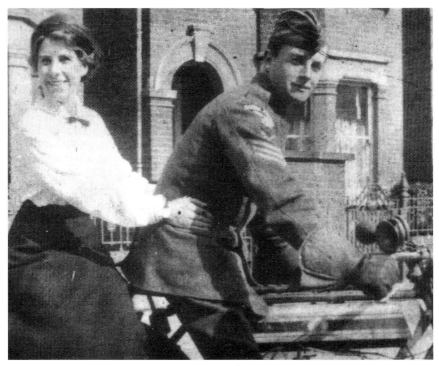

Flight Sergeant J. T. B. McCudden on a motorbike with his sister Mary. Comparing McCudden's and von Richthofen's combat reports there is no doubt that these two were in action on 27 December. As for von Richthofen, McCudden was, in reality, 'one who got away'.

Captain J. T. B McCudden at the height of his fighting powers. He received the VC, DSO & Bar, MC & Two Bars, MM and *CdG*, becoming one of the top-scoring aces of the RFC/RAF. His untimely death in a flying accident on 9 July 1918 robbed the RAF of an outstanding airman. Had von Richthofen shot him down on 27 December, the name of James McCudden would have passed into obscurity.

Manfred von Richthofen wearing the *Pour le Mérite* that he was awarded on 12 January 1917. This portrait, along with many similar ones, was sold as a postcard all over German during the war years. He was not alone in this; all German war heroes could expect to be treated similarly.

Those interested in von Richthofen will know of his obsession with collecting souvenirs from his downed opponents. As most Allied aircraft came down inside German territory it was not overly difficult to have them collected. There are many pictures of Manfred's souvenirs which he kept in his rooms on the various airfields he operated from. Not so well known is that this habit was started by Boelcke or, at least, someone started it for him. This cabinet shows a number of Boelcke's souvenirs, including the serial number 2287, taken from an RE.7 of 12 Squadron which he downed on 12 January 1916, his eighth victory.

This same cabinet stands on the right, while to the left are more trophies, including a propeller and the fuselage of a Nieuport Scout. His portrait, edged in black, indicates that this picture was taken after his death in action.

Chapter Two

Staffelführer

Jasta 11 was based at la Brayelles, near Douai, opposite the British front. In 1909 there had been a large aviation race meeting held there. Today most of it lies beneath a huge Renault factory. *Jasta 11* had a few rudimentary buildings and a large wooden hangar, and some mud. It would remain here until mid–April.

Manfred had about a dozen pilots under his command, several of whom would become well known over the next months as they held their new commander in some esteem and he in turn encouraged them, just as Boelcke had encouraged him. A number of them started to perform well almost immediately while others, who did not come up to his standard, were usually posted away, leaving room for other rising stars he came across to be posted in.

After Manfred had downed the unit's first victory, an FE.8 pusher, piloted by Second Lieutenant John Hay, he bagged two more and then *Vizefeldwebel* (sergeant major) Sebastian Festner scored his first on 5 February. Gradually, over the following weeks, others began to score, interspersed with victories by Manfred. Those who began to shine were *Leutnants* Emil Schäfer, Karl Allmenröder, Kurt Wolff and Festner.

Following his nineteenth victory on 1 February, a BE.2d, Manfred went on leave. It came at a time when the German fighter force was starting to have problems with the Albatros D.II. His own machine had suffered a cracked wing the previous day, so that on 1 February he began flying a Halberstadt Scout and would do so for some weeks. He returned on the 13th, and on the 14th downed two British aircraft,

BE.2c machines from No. 2 Squadron, one at noon, the other at 1645 that afternoon. On the 4th, Manfred scored twice, a BE.2d from No. 2 Squadron in the late morning, followed by a Sopwith 1½ Strutter, of 43 Squadron, in the late afternoon. All four crew members died.

Then, in early March, Manfred's brother Lothar arrived. He, too, had been a cavalry officer pre-war, serving with the 4th Dragoons but, following Manfred's lead, had transferred to aviation in late 1915. For a year he had served as an observer with *KG4*, then trained as a pilot and Manfred got him assigned to *Jasta 11*. He scored his first victory on 28 March, like Manfred's an FE.2b.

The day of Lothar's arrival – the 6th – turned out to be a bad one for Manfred because he was shot down. Although he shot down victim number twenty-four that afternoon, he had been lucky to survive an encounter that morning. FE.8 machines from No. 40 Squadron were on an offensive patrol and pilots of *Jasta 11* engaged them above Givenchy-en-Gohelle at 1050 hours (1150 German time). The start of the action had been against Sopwith 1½ Strutters of 43 Squadron, the FE.8s diving to their rescue. Closing in behind one Sopwith, Manfred failed to see an FE.8 slip in behind him and open fire. Manfred heard a terrific bang followed by the stench of petrol. His fuel tank had been holed.

An airman's worst fear was fire and Manfred was lucky that the machine did not immediately turn into a ball of flame, sending him down to a painful death. He quickly turned off the engine and, with petrol still squirting between his legs, began to head down, leaving a trail of vaporised petrol behind him. As the battle continued above him, he saw one Sopwith falling in flames, shot down by Schäffer, then saw one of his own pilots spinning down before pulling out to make a forced landing.

Manfred made a dead-stick landing near Henin-Liétard, climbed out and inspected the damage. The other Halberstadt he had seen land was flown by *Leutnant* Eduard Lübbert, who had suffered a slight wound but had also landed safely. Two of 40 Squadron's pilots put in claims for German fighters shot down, Captain R. Gregory and Lieutenant E. L. Benbow. Benbow claimed a 'flamer' that might have been von Richthofen going down leaving what may have looked like a smoke trail. Gregory said his went down 'out of control' and was probably Lübbert. Out of control victory claims were more or less 'probables' where a crash had not been witnessed, but appeared inevitable. Often it wasn't.

Manfred laid himself down and went to sleep while he awaited rescue, which came in the form of some German soldiers who took him to their positions and gave him lunch. He was then driven back to Brayelles. As if it were a build-up to what was going to be a massive scoring rate in April, the rest of March produced twenty-three further victories for *Jasta 11*. They met up with the FE.8s of 40 Squadron again on the 9th, this time downing four of them, Wolff and Allmenröder one each, Schäffer two. Other FEs were shot about but got back over the lines. Manfred shot down a DH.2 of 29 Squadron at noon. Only Schäffer suffered a forced landing in the 40 Squadron fight but was unhurt.

At this period both Richthofens, Wolff, Schäffer, and Allmenröder were all scoring freely, and by the end of the month, *Jasta 11*'s victories totalled thirty-six. Lübbert, shot down again on the 30th, was the *Jasta*'s sole fatal casualty.

* * *

By this time Manfred von Richthofen was fast becoming an established air fighter, his reputation growing. He was also learning how to achieve success in air combat and, somewhat like Oswald Boelcke, thought about things rather than engage in combat with little regard for his own safety. There were no end of heroic but foolhardy fighter aces on both sides, who merely engaged in combat in the hope they would succeed, and with the feeling that they would always survive.

Richthofen, now being a commander, and especially when he later commanded four *Jagdstaffeln* in the summer of 1917, generally selected young men for his group who seemed eager to learn and, with relatively little experience, could be trained the way he preferred. He acknowledged that he was not the greatest pilot; his success was his ability to quickly size up a situation, and being a good shot. As he later wrote:

> On flying itself I put considerably less value. I shot down my first twenty [Allied aircraft] at a time when flying was very difficult for me. It makes no difference if one is an aerial artist. Moreover, I prefer those men who can make left turns but who dash to meet the enemy to those fancy flyers who attack too cautiously.
>
> I forbid the following practices over the aerodrome. Looping, spinning, banking at low level; we do not need aerial acrobats but men who dash at the enemy. I do require target practice while aloft and at high speeds, and tight turns at full speed.

If a new pilot to his group did not appear to be shaping up quickly that man was soon posted to another unit, or back to a training school. He also required discipline in the air. He, and other successful unit leaders, encouraged those who could engage and shoot straight to lead attacks on enemy formations, using their skill to down the opposition in the first pass, before a general *mêlée* developed. It was a sound tactic which brought results.

Richthofen did not like defensive patrols, which he deemed wasted time and petrol. He liked his airfields as close to the front lines as possible where he would await reports of British aircraft actually crossing the front lines before he gave to order to take off. Often he and his men would scour the sky above the lines with powerful telescopes in order to identify numbers, types and direction, before getting into their machines.

He generally had his pilots ready for immediate take off soon after daybreak, each man dressed and prepared for action, the mechanics keeping the aircraft engines warmed up. Once in the air, there was no particular formation keeping; he merely led his men as if it was a hunt. He always tried to attack an opponent from the rear and found that most pilots, when attacked from behind, banked away, so he would throttle back and make a tight turn to follow. If he attacked a two-seater he would try to knock out the gunner/observer first, taking care not to overshoot, putting himself in danger from a front gun.

His view was that his squadron's purpose was to keep the air above German soldiers and trenches clear of being molested by enemy aircraft, and in this way he was able to support and protect the men on the ground. If he had a choice he would go for the two-seat observation reconnaissance machines, infantry flyers or photographic aircraft. It was these aircraft that were the danger to the troops on the ground. It has been said that he chose these machines as they were easier to shoot down, but two-seaters could be dangerous. In any event, as was proved, he could outfight all types of British single-seaters, and several pilots in these fighters were well tried and tested in their own right.

He advocated the need to break off combat if things got too tough. His doctrine was 'A live pilot is better than a dead hero'. There was always tomorrow. He rarely took chances. He never engaged in anti-balloon raids for they could prove dangerous, nor did he involve himself or his men in attacking ground targets, troops or trenches. He always seemed able to appraise a situation and act accordingly, and rarely made mistakes. He only made two serious mistakes: one caused him a serious head wound, the other his life.

* * *

The first Bristol Fighter (BF.2a) squadron arrived in France on 8 March 1917. This was No. 48 Squadron, commanded by Major A. V. Bettington. Based at Bertangles, it began a period of preparation for front-line flying. This took almost a month because of poor weather and also, being a new type in France, time was taken to ensure everyone was well versed in what the squadron needed to achieve.

The Bristol was a two-seater, with a pilot and observer. Both had access to machine guns, the pilot a single front-firing one, set to fire through the propeller, while the observer had a moveable Lewis gun on a mounting in the rear cockpit for defensive fire to the rear. Unfortunately, the original concept was that if a formation of Bristols became engaged, they would close up for mutual protection. As Bristol crews discovered on operations, their aircraft were so agile they could act more like single-seat fighters with the bonus of a rear gunner defending the rear while the pilot could concentrate on attacking hostile aircraft from the front.

On 5 April the squadron was deemed ready and sent out a patrol of six aircraft led by the senior flight commander, Captain William Leefe Robinson VC. Robinson had won his Victoria Cross for bringing down a German airship over north London in September 1916.

Richthofen with four of his men found the patrol, attacked, and within a short space of time had shot down four of the Bristols. Two fell to Manfred, while Sebastian Festner shot down Robinson, George Simon claiming the fourth. Robinson became a prisoner and survived the war, only to die during the influenza pandemic on the last day of 1918.

After the action with the new British type, von Richthofen reported that little need be feared from it, and indeed, 48 Squadron suffered further casualties during April. Lothar, Schäfer and Wolff downed three more on 11 April, Lothar getting another on the 13th. RFC Headquarters were shocked by this as high hopes had been placed upon the Bristol. It took time to adopt new tactics but it was not long before the 'Brisfits' became aircraft to be feared.

The coveted *Pour le Mérite*, Germany's highest award for bravery. Manfred received his on 12 January 1917 following his sixteenth aerial victory, and as he was given command of *Jasta 11*.

Second Lieutenant John Hay of 40 Squadron became Manfred's first victory leading *Jasta 11*, on 23 January 1917. Hay's FE.8 caught fire and went down, its pilot jumping out rather than face the flames. It was the day after the Australian's twenty-eighth birthday.

Manfred was flying this Albatros D.III (789/17) when he shot down John Hay. He switched to the Halberstadt Scout at the end of January as the Albatros machines were having wing problems. His aircraft were now painted mostly red, although the rudder and wheel covers were white. The cowling and top of the engine were bare metal.

The Halberstadt D.II scout. Manfred began using this type of machine following problems with the early Albatros D-types during February 1917.

Wreckage of Manfred's twenty-third victory, a Sopwith 1½ Strutter of 43 Squadron near Acheville on 4 March 1917. Lieutenants W. Reid and H. Green perished.

Brother Lothar von Richthofen arrived on *Jasta 11* in early March 1917, to become deputy commander. Within two months he had scored sufficient victories to merit the award of the Blue Max.

The British FE.8 pusher fighter. Aircraft like this with 40 Squadron got into a fight with *Jasta 11* on 6 March, resulting in Manfred being shot about and, with his petrol tank holed, forced towards the ground. No. 40 Squadron was led by Captain W. Robert Gregory, but it was Lieutenant E. L. Benbow who scored the damaging hits.

Captain Edwin Benbow MC. In 1918 he was a flight commander with 85 Squadron but was killed in action on 30 May, having achieved eight victories in combat, all with 40 Squadron.

Leutnant Hans Lübbert was also shot up in the 6 March fight by Captain Gregory and, with a slight wound, also went down to make a forced landing. By chance, Gregory and Lübbert met again on 30 March; this time the German pilot did not survive the encounter.

Captain W. R. Gregory MC, was Irish, son of the Right Honourable Sir William Gregory KCMG. Educated at Harrow and Oxford he had married and had a son. Born 20 May 1881 he was aged thirty-three when war came. As well as winning the MC, the French also awarded him the *Legion d'honneur and Croix de Guerre.* He later commanded 66 Squadron, taking it to Italy in late 1917. Sadly he was killed in a flying accident on 25 January 1918.

Jasta 11 met 40 Squadron on several occasions. On 9 March Kurt Wolff downed this FE.8, whose pilot was captured. It was not a good day for 40 Squadron, as they lost five FEs in this fight.

Even before the Battle of Arras began, *Jasta 11* had a successful encounter on 5 April. No. 48 Squadron had recently arrived in France, equipped with the new Bristol 2a fighter, designed as a two-seater for air fighting as well as reconnaissance. Its senior flight commander was Captain W. Leefe Robinson VC, who had received his high decoration for bringing down the German airship SL11. The BF.2b (an improvement on the 2a) was to become a formidable fighting machine once it was realised how to use front and rear guns effectively but, at this early stage, the tactic, if engaged, was to remain in formation and let the observers in the rear cockpit ward off attacks from the rear. This played into the German pilots' hands and, in this action, four of the six 'Brisfits' were shot down. Manfred shot down A3340, seen here, which was destroyed by fire, started by the wounded pilot after he'd landed and got his mortally wounded observer out.

Manfred then turned his attention to A3343, forcing it to land near Cuincy where the crew were taken prisoner. The encounters were not helped by later reports from the returning observers that they had suffered gun jams and frozen oil.

Line-up of *Jasta 11*'s Albatros D.IIIs at Douai, the mechanics awaiting the arrival of their pilots. Richthofen's all-red machine is second from the front. Its fuselage and tail crosses have been largely obscured by the red paint.

Like Boelcke before him, Manfred also collected souvenirs from his downed opponents, and had them displayed in his room wherever he was based. This picture shows the most tangible proof of a kill is a serial number cut from the crashed aircraft, or perhaps the rotary engine made into a light fitting from the ceiling. N5193, top left is from a Pup, downed on 4 January 1917; A3340, to its right, is from a BF.2a shot down on 5 April; below them is 6618, BE.12 on 7 October 1916, and 6232, a BE.2d, 11 March 1917; 6697, FE.2b, 24 January 1917, and 6580, a BE.12, 16 October 1916; while below these is 4997, an FE.2b, 13 April 1917. Above his picture is A5446, from an FE.2b, 20 December 1916. On the right is A/1108, a 1½ Strutter, 4 March 1917, and, below, A6382 comes from FE.2d, 3 April 1917.

Chapter Three

Bloody April

By April, with the winter weather finally starting to clear, both Allied and German armies were preparing for a spring offensive, but the British got in first. Their attack began on Easter Monday, 9 April 1917. The artillery had started shelling the German positions the previous evening and, at dawn, in spite of early mist followed by wind and snow showers, the British troops went forward. In the air there was going to be a mighty array of RFC aircraft flying reconnaissance, bombing, artillery direction and other support missions. On the other side of the lines, the *Jasta* pilots on numerous airfields had been waiting for just such an opportunity. Over recent months, since the *Jastas* had begun forming, all that was needed was the chance to meet the *Englanders* (the Germans also referred to RFC/RNAS pilots as the *English Lords*) and test their new tactics and aircraft in combat.

The *Jasta* cannot be compared exactly to the British squadron in terms of numbers. Generally a *Jasta* had fewer pilots, in some cases, little more than would number in a British flight. Whereas a British squadron would operate in flight strength of about five or six, or perhaps, in an important operation, in squadron strength of all three flights, the *Jasta* would operate with its full complement that might average eight to ten pilots, led by its leader. If that leader was good, such as von Richthofen, that would be the norm, whereas in other *Jastas*, where perhaps a *staffelführer* felt someone else would be better at leading, that other man would be assigned. As the *Jasta* war developed, the main tactic was to have one main leader, whether it be the *staffelführer* or not, and it would be he who would commence an attack upon Allied aircraft.

This leader would have already proved himself as being able to down enemy aircraft, due to being a good shot, a good pilot, and able to control things in the air. The RFC fighter units on the other hand might be led by a flight commander of course, but when action came it was often every man for himself, and everybody bundled in. The German leader led an attack in the knowledge that his men were protecting his tail, thereby allowing him to concentrate fully upon the target ahead without worrying that some enemy pilot was sneaking up behind him. Only when an air fight was really underway did the other pilots get a chance to go after some opponent, by which time the aircraft might well be spread all over the sky. In this way, too, it became a case of just one or two, perhaps three, *Jasta* pilots with rising scores of victories making the kills, while the rest occasionally managed to notch up a victim or two.

In the case of some other *Jastas*, notably *Jasta 11*, they began to have several pilots with increasing scores. By the start of the Battle of Arras, *Jasta 11* under von Richthofen had achieved some sixty victories. Manfred's score now stood at thirty-nine, while Schäfer had fourteen, Allmenröder five, Wolff eight and Festner seven. And they had not lost a single pilot in action. By April 1917, thirty-seven *Jastas* had been created.

April 1917 turned out to be a glorious time for the new *Jasta* pilots. There were so many targets it was difficult for many pilots not to shoot down RFC and RNAS aircraft almost at will. It proved to be the Allied airmen's costliest month in terms of casualties, a month that would not be matched until September 1918. The RFC called it 'Bloody April' in consequence. Manfred's *Jasta 11* claimed a total of eighty-nine victories, the top-scoring unit, and the four top aces also came from *Jasta 11*, Wolff with twenty-three, Manfred with twenty-two,

Schäfer twenty-one and Lothar von Richthofen, fifteen. Even Festner was eighth on the list with ten.

Lothar's rise was amazing and, included in his fifteen kills in April, he had scored doubles on the 11th, 13th, 14th, 29th and 30th. He became the *Jasta*'s acting commander in Manfred's absence and on 10 May received the Hohenzollern House Order. Manfred described his brother as a bit of a butcher when it came to air combat, always attacking aggressively rather than sizing up the opposition beforehand. It was this that often brought good scores but, by the same token, led to him being seriously wounded on 13 May. By that time he had increased his personal victory total to twenty-four. The following day came the announcement of Lothar's award of the *Pour le Mérite*. The wound, inflicted by ground-fire, put him out of action until late September and then, being given command of *Jasta 11*, he had to spend more time in administrative duties than in the air.

Jasta 11 also moved its base in this month, moving to Roucourt near Bohain, south-east of Douai, on the 15th, where it would remain until 9 June, when it moved again, to Harlebecke. Roucourt had better accommodation than Brayelles, in fact a French château, from where, it was only a short walk or drive to the airfield. Another significant event that occurred in April was that the *Jasta* brought its total victories to one hundred on the 22nd. Four victories were claimed this day, one by Manfred, one by Schäffer, and two by Wolff, but it was Wolff who got the hundredth. Schäffer received the Blue Max on the 26th, while Wolff would receive his on 4 May. At the end of 'Bloody April', *Jasta 11* had been credited with 125 Allied aircraft shot down.

April ended with Manfred downing five enemy aircraft in two days. He was about to go on leave on 1 May, leaving Lothar in command, but he had a couple of days left, and undoubtedly was aware that, with a personal score of forty-seven, it would be nice to return home with a nice round fifty. He got number forty-eight on the 28th, a BE.2e of 13 Squadron.

The crew of this BE had been happily ranging artillery fire for an hour along the XVII Corps' front. Being engrossed, both the pilot, Lieutenant R. W. Follit, and observer, Second Lieutenant F. J. Kirkham, failed to see the attack coming. Frederick Kirkham had been occupied with his Morse key, sending ranging corrections to the gun batteries they were working with, and his pilot, seated in the rear cockpit of course, was hit in the back during von Richthofen's first pass. Kirkham quickly manned his machine gun to engage the German Albatros, fully aware that with his pilot seemingly mortally wounded, his own death was imminent. However, he maintained fire on the Albatros as the BE went down, von Richthofen continuing to fire into the British machine.

With extreme luck, despite having several bullets tear through his flying coat, the BE hit some trees, near a German artillery position. Petrol was everywhere, but German soldiers cut both men out of the wreckage, and they were taken to the nearest aid station where Follit died. He had only married the previous year and the Germans gave Kirkham the dead man's wedding ring which he returned to his widow after the war.

A few days later, his injuries attended to, Kirkham began his journey into captivity, but via *Jasta 11*'s airfield. Richthofen happened to be absent during this visit, but Kirkham was told he had been downed by the Red Baron during his time with the *Jasta*.

However, the events of 29 April are worth recording in more detail, especially as we have an account by one of the RFC pilots involved, and the only one to survive. Manfred's score at this time was forty-eight, and he was due for a rest. Returning home with fifty victories would be an achievement, and as it happens, he downed an impressive four British aeroplanes. The first of these he achieved shortly after midday, while the other three occurred in the late afternoon and early evening.

But it is the events of the first encounter that are recorded here in more detail. His combat report, or the translation of it, records the time as 1205 hours above the swamps of Lécluse, east of Arras and south of Douai, and states:

> With several of my gentlemen, I attacked an English Spad group consisting of three machines. The plane I singled out broke to pieces whilst curving, and plunged, burning, into the swamp near Lécluse.

According to the survivor of this encounter, Lieutenant W. N. Hamilton, the British patrol was not an ordinary one, but one especially ordered to deal with the Baron and his pilots. On the face of it, this does sound a tad far-fetched but we must assume this to be his understanding. Hamilton had been born in Egypt and came to England to be educated when he was six. As a young man he had gone to India to work, but returned soon after the war began, enlisting in the Northumberland Fusiliers and, following action during the Somme offensive, transferred to the Royal Flying Corps and became a pilot. Once trained, he was posted to 19 Squadron in February 1917. After the war he wrote down his experiences of 29 April. He began the day working with his mechanics on his machine gun. His commanding officer was Major H. D. Harvey-Kelly DSO, recorded as being the first RFC pilot to land in France following the declaration of war.

> Harvey-Kelly came to me and said that Wing was [in] 'hot-action' about Richthofen's Circus having been seen over Douai and wanted three Spads to go up and deal with them. Owing to the machines of the other flights either being away on patrol or the [other] not ready, [H-K] was ordered to send away the four of C Flight.

In the ordinary course of events, the other [flight] should have taken the job since we had already done one patrol that day but as the matter was urgent I agreed to take my pilots up again. At that moment Harvey-Kelly decided that he himself would go instead of me but I declined to be left behind, [so] I detached one of my pilots (Harding) to remain behind and let the Major have his machine.

Harvey-Kelly and myself took off and formed together [saw a third Spad, still on the ground] making no attempt to follow us, so we presumed something had gone wrong, so went off by ourselves. Contrary to the information contained in the RAF casualty report, we were not on any particular patrol but chased about looking for the Circus. We had been in the air about two hours when a third Spad joined us and judging from the markings I concluded Applin had eventually got away and found us. This was particularly praiseworthy as Applin had had very little experience over the lines and it required considerable pluck for a more or less raw pilot to search for us by himself, forty miles behind the German lines. He took up station on my right rear as we always flew. In this formation it was the duty of the No. 3 to protect 1 and 2 from attack from behind.

Soon after Applin joined us we sighted the Circus about 1,000 feet below us, eighteen fighter planes and flying more or less in line ahead stylish echelon. As we were then only 4,000 feet up I did not expect Harvey-Kelly would attack but at the same moment we noticed six Triplanes (RNAS) flying towards us. Harvey-Kelly gave the signal to attack but the Triplanes sheered off and left us to it. Harvey-Kelly had already turned and dived at the tail Hun and I was diving to attack the centre machine so as to break their formation and prevent the leading machine getting above us. Applin was following us when I saw him stall on his turn and go down in a spin and then burst into flames. I looked up and saw that Richthofen, who had been cruising about 2,000 feet above his Circus (his usual position) had evidently shot Applin down, as he had swooped away immediately after I left him alone and carried out my original plans of attacking the centre machine, noticing as I did so, that Harvey-Kelly had apparently accounted for two Huns and was pretty busy with four or five more.

I joined battle a second or two later (our position at that time was somewhere over Epinoy). I didn't see Harvey-Kelly again as I was fully occupied with my little bunch and carried on a running fight till over Douai but my gun jammed. I made a rapid examination and found my cursed drum had forced a double feed so that there was nothing to be done except get away. I 'split-arsed' to get to the lines when they managed to hit my main tank which, being under my feet, was force-fed into the engine. Of course the moment the pressure was released my engine stopped and as it stopped on a turn, I stalled and spun. I got her out almost immediately, switched onto my gravity tank and dived to pick up my engine again. In doing so, however, I naturally lost a bit of height and also cooled my engine to such an extent that she was not giving me full revs and I was now much lower than my opponents, in addition to being below them.

I held my bus down to keep up speed and steered for our lines but very soon had four of the enemy on my tail. At least one was on my tail, one above and one on each side behind. They made pretty good shooting and managed to shoot away all my instruments and most of my struts and flying wires, so that before long I was practically flying a monoplane as my bottom planes were flapping. Had I been flying any machine other than a Spad it would have crumpled up but the Spad, having no dihedral, the main span of the top plane was solid right through which no doubt saved my life.

I had got down to about 300 feet when they holed my gravity tank and my engine stopped for good. I made a good landing just behind Oppy Wood, about a kilometre short of the lines and while the Huns on the ground were running up to secure me I endeavoured to fire my bus. During this time the four Huns in the air (one Richthofen's brother, flying a red-nosed Albatros) continued firing at me. Owing to having no petrol left I was unsuccessful in firing my bus but I saw her hit by our own guns soon after so that she was completely destroyed.

I learnt later that Applin was dead and that Harvey-Kelly died in hospital three days later from head wounds.

Hamilton remained a prisoner until the war ended, being repatriated on the last day of 1918. He had been Lothar's thirteenth victory. Hubert Dunsterville Harvey-Kelly fell to Kurt Wolff, his twenty-fifth kill.

What the exact circumstances of this patrol were is difficult to say for certain. On the face of it, an experienced leader like Harvey-Kelly would not, in the ordinary turn of events, have gone up after a formation of von Richthofen's *Jasta 11*, with just two pilots, one being very inexperienced. However, it is known that his squadron at Vert Galant was expecting a visit later that day by Major General Hugh Trenchard CB DSO, General Officer Commanding the RFC in France (and ADC to the King), with his influential adjutant, Captain the Honourable Maurice Baring.

Commanding officers of RFC squadrons at this time were not required to fly on operations, far less lead a small patrol. It is also difficult to be sure if he even knew the reported German fighter formation was von Richthofen's bunch. Richthofen's fighters were not the only ones that had some red on their aeroplanes. Perhaps the myth was born and grew over the years, and Harvey-Kelly merely went up so that his three-man patrol might help clear the air above the front of enemy aircraft. Perhaps Hamilton wanted to record a better story of his demise. In his post-war story he had mentioned that, between them, Harvey-Kelly and he had accounted for five Huns before being shot down. *Jasta 11* had no casualties.

* * *

At 1655 pm Manfred made it fifty by downing a FE.2d of 18 Squadron, near Pariville. Again he was with five of his pilots, and engaged five FEs. Manfred said his opponents handled themselves well but, getting in behind the big FE, it was always difficult for the observer in the front cockpit to fire back at an attacker. It did not take long for the FE to catch fire and go down, both occupants falling or jumping out of the burning wreck. The sergeant pilot was nineteen years old, his corporal gunner only eighteen.

About two hours later, having landed and refuelled, Manfred and Lothar took off to patrol along the front and met two British aircraft from 12 Squadron on artillery directing work. Manfred attacked one, which lost its wings and crashed near Rouex. The crew were aged twenty-five and twenty-one. Lothar shot down the other which fell north-east of Monchy-le-Preux. Both occupants died and both were nineteen years of age.

Following this action, both brothers were attacked by some Sopwith Triplanes from 1 and 8 Naval Squadrons near Henin-Liétard, accompanied by Spads of 19 Squadron and Nieuports of 40 Squadron. Being outnumbered, the brothers made a quick exit, but not before Manfred attacked one of the Naval aeroplanes and set it on fire. It fell burning, taking its twenty-seven-year old Canadian, Flight Sub-Lieutenant A. E. Cuzner, with it. Lothar did not make a claim.

Manfred took his leave and headed for Germany where he arrived in the knowledge that he had not only surpassed Boelcke's victory score by a dozen, but that he was Germany's ace of aces. He had recently been awarded a number of decorations, and more were to follow. On 13 April he had received the Württenburg Military Merit Order, while on the 16th he had received the Knight's Cross of the Saxon Military St Henry Order. On 9 May came the Knight's Cross with Swords, of the Ducal Saxe-Ernestine House Order, from the Duchy of Coburg and Gotha. Unbeknown to him he had also been nominated for the Knight's Cross of the Military Max-Joseph Order, Bavaria's highest award, but it was not approved as the specific rules governing such an award did not cover someone who hadn't defended a fortress or taken one. Instead the Bavarians gave him their Military Merit Order, 3rd Class, with Crown and Swords, which presumably satisfied everyone.

Jasta 11 had a number of successful pilots, all achieving some measure of success, especially during April 1917. Manfred is in the cockpit, while Schäffer sits on the wing. Others from L to R are: Allmenröder, Hans Hintsch, Sebastian Festner, Emil Schäffer, Kurt Wolff, Georg Simon, Otto Brauneck; in front: Karl Esser, Constantin Krefft, Lothar von Richthofen.

Manfred, on the left, while talking to Krefft, Wolff and Brauneck, on the front steps of the château at Roucourt, April 1917.

Manfred's father, Major Albrecht von Richthofen, visiting his sons and taking a photo opportunity on the rear steps of Roucourt château, in April 1917. In front: Simon, Wolff, Manfred, Major von Richthofen, Krefft and Hintsch; Rear: Allmenröder, Lothar, Wolfgang Plüschow, von Hartmann.

Karl Allmenröder and Manfred discussing the coming day's operations. April 1917. The airfield is off to the right, the château within the trees on the left.

Lothar in the cockpit of his Albatros Scout, while Allmenröder gives him last minute advice. The ladders were necessary for pilots to climb up into the cockpit. At this stage Lothar's aircraft carried a large red stripe round the fuselage aft of the cockpit.

More deep discussion, with Wolff, a visiting Austrian, Krefft and Manfred, looking rather quizzically at the man holding the camera.

Another smiling Manfred, and a slight bow from the waist. He is greeting Hauptmann Viktor Carganico, who had been with Manfred in *BAO*, before commanding a two-seater *Abteilung*.

A happy Manfred astride another form of transport, this time smiling at the camera.
Note another use of ladders, for mechanics to have access to the aeroplane's engine.

Lieutenant E. C. E. Derwin and his observer, Gunner H. Pierson, were shot down on 11 April, coming down in the front-line area, so Manfred was unable to discover who the occupants were. Derwin was killed in the action, but his wounded observer was rescued by front-line troops and he survived. More significantly, it was Manfred's fortieth victory, so he was now level with his mentor, Oswald Boelcke. In our book *Under the Guns of the Red Baron* Hal Giblin and I failed to find a picture of Derwin, but this has now been rectified, Derwin being shown here as he passed his flying tests to gain his licence on 29 July 1915.

On 14 April Manfred shot down Lieutenant W. O. Russell of 60 Squadron who was flying a Nieuport 17 Scout. It had been Russell's second patrol and his machine had already been damaged during an attack on a German two-seater moments earlier, so these two facts gave him little chance against von Richthofen. The twenty-four-year old Londoner did, however, get down and become a prisoner.

More visitors. Manfred (on the right) with Hauptmann Paul von Osterroht. He had been Manfred's pilot during his time as an observer, during their *BAO* days. At this stage he was commanding *Jasta 12* but fell in combat on 23 April.

Sketches of *Jasta 11* pilots by Professor Arnold Busch, in July 1917. Clockwise from the top: Karl von Schönebeck, Alfred Neiderhoff, Busch, Gisbert Groos, Otto Brauneck, Eberhardt Stapenhörst, Constantin Krefft, Karl Meyer, Lothar vR, Kurt Wolff, Wilhelm Reinhard, Joachim Wolff, Franz Müller, Eberhardt Eberhard Mohnicke, Manfred vR (middle), Wilhelm Bockelmann, Karl Bodenschatz, Karl Schäffer.

Jasta 11. L to R: von Hartmann, Wolfgang Plüschow, Constantin Krefft, Georg Simon, Kurt Wolff, Karl Effers, Manfred vR, Lothar vR, Hans Hintsch, Otto Brauneck, Matthof, Karl Allmenröder.

Kurt Wolff (centre) used to fly with a lucky stocking on his head. Here, with Constantin Krefft on the left, Karl Allmenröder is having some fun with him.

Another visit by von Richthofen senior. L to r: Krefft, von Althaus, Manfred, Erwin Böhme and Major von Richthofen. *Oberleutnant* Ernst Freiherr von Althaus was leader of *Jasta 10*, having been a successful Fokker pilot with *Kek* Vaux in 1916. Böhme, of course, had been with Manfred in *Jasta 2* and was now commanding it.

Another picture taken during this same visit. Otto Brauneck, Manfred, Major von Richthofen, Böhme, Krefft. Although a pilot, Constantin Krefft was also the unit's Technical Officer.

Lieutenant R. W. Follit of 13 Squadron, seated in a car with his future wife, Lilian Watkins, in the autumn of 1914. She received his wedding ring after the war, returned by her husband's observer upon his release from prison camp.

The action on 29 April, the day prior to Manfred's departure on leave, when he, in company with his brother, and Kurt Wolff, with a couple of others, fell upon three Spads of 19 Squadron and shot them all down. The Spads were led by Major H. D. Harvey-Kelly DSO, credited with being the first RFC pilot to land in France after war had been declared in August 1914. He died under the guns of Wolff, the ace's twenty-fourth victory.

Lieutenant F. J. Kirkham, Follitt's observer on 28 April 1917. He fought the Baron all the way down until their BE crashed into some trees. He had previously been with the Royal Field Artillery, transferring to the RFC after five months in France to become an observer.

Lieutenant W. N. Hamilton managed to get down during this action to be taken into captivity, shot down by Lothar von Richthofen for his thirteenth victory.

Lieutenant Richard Applin, from Cleveden, Somerset, was brought down by Manfred – his forty-ninth victory. He had joined 19 Squadron on 14 March but had not been allowed to fly the Spad operationally until 3 April. This twenty-two-year old, only child of a schoolteacher father, had lasted just twenty-six days. Manfred was flying Albatros D.III, 2253/17.

Chapter Four

Jagdgeschwader Nr. 1

By the end of April von Richthofen and his *Jasta 11* were masters of the air above the Western Front. The unit's total claims had reached 125 and some of its stars had been rewarded. On 26 April Karl Emil Schäfer received the *Pour le Mérite*, his total at this date being twenty-three. His daring had almost been his undoing, especially on the occasion he engaged a British aeroplane at around 200 feet in bad weather and was hit by ground fire. Forced to make a crash-landing near to the trenches, he came under intense fire from British soldiers and had to make a mad rush, from shell hole to shell hole, crater to crater, to evade death. Another reward was to be given command of *Jasta 28*.

On 4 May Kurt Wolff received the Blue Max, his score having reached twenty-nine on the 1st. (On 29 April he had scored three victories, including Harvey-Kelly, the CO of 19 Squadron mentioned earlier.) Ten days later, 14 May, Lothar von Richthofen also received the Blue Max. On the 13th he had downed his twenty-fourth victory although he had been wounded and sent off to hospital.

* * *

The next Blue Max winner in *Jasta 11* was Karl Allmenröder, on 14 June. His score at the time was twenty-six. All four men had, of course, been awarded the Hohenzollern House Order, the usual prerequisite for the Blue Max. Another excellent air fighter who had joined *Jasta 11* on 10 April had been *Leutnant* Otto Brauneck, whose score stood at six by the end of May. However, the great Karl Schäfer had fallen. His death on 5 June hit the *Jasta* hard. He had achieved thirty victories, the last seven whilst leading his *Jasta 28*. It is generally accepted he was shot down by the FE.2 crew of No. 20 Squadron, Lieutenants H. L. Satchell and T. A. M. S. Lewis.

Meanwhile, Manfred had still been on leave and did not return until 17 June, by which time *Jasta 11* had moved to Harlebecke. Lothar had been in temporary command until he was wounded, and then Allmenröder had taken over.

One reason for Manfred's leave was that the German Emperor, Kaiser Wilhelm II, had asked to see him. Manfred first attended General Headquarters on 2 May to be briefed, and was then flown to Germany in a DFW two-seater piloted by Krefft. They arrived in Cologne with all manner of people wanting to see and meet him. Next he met General Ernst von Hoeppner, General Officer Commanding the Air Service, and included in his visit was a tour of the Air Service Headquarters. He also attended a meeting with Field Marshal Paul von Hindenburg, the Chief of the General Staff and his assistant, General Erich Ludendorff.

His meetings with the Kaiser and the Empress went well enough, the latter taking place at the Empress's Bad Homburg residence. Krefft flew him there too. The visit home then included some hunting in the Black Forest. Other things he did while in Germany included inspection of new aircraft designs at Alderdorf, no doubt seeing the improved Albatros D.V, working on the book he had been asked to write, and further hunting on the Pless Estates, where he was able to shoot bison.

By mid-June it was time to return to France. No doubt some discussions had taken place at Air HQ concerning the possibility of forming a new unit, by combining several *Jastas* into a single entity under the leadership of one commander. To this end, *Jasta 11* was to be combined with *Jasta 4*, *Jasta 6* and *Jasta 10* to form Royal Prussian *Jagdgeschwader Nr. I* on 26 June. Later in the war, four other *Jagdgeschwaderen* were formed, II and III in February 1918, a *Marine Jagdgeschwader* in September and, finally, *Bavarian Jagdgeschwader Nr. IV* in October 1918.

By this time Manfred had been painting his aircraft red, and had become known as the Red Baron. German pilots were encouraged to paint their aircraft in bright colours and designs and it suited their purpose to do so. Individual pilots could be more easily identified in the air, and Manfred's all-red fighter was an easy rallying point if the formation became split up during a combat. Not that his machine was always totally red. Generally the only time he had an all-red machine was whilst fighting over an active battle front, where any machine he shot down became inaccessible for inspection in the battle zone. Front-line troops might see his actions and the victory could, hopefully, be attributed to him by being confirmed from the ground. On other occasions, only parts of his fighter were painted red. Other pilots in the *Jasta* also had red-painted machines but with sections in a variety of colours, such as yellow for Lothar, green for Wolff and so on, making them easy to identify in the air while maintaining an overall unit identity.

The formation of *JGI*, which was tasked with moving from one front-line hotspot to another, and the colourful decoration on the aircraft, brought the title of Circus into aviation history. In time it became known as the Richthofen Circus.

As the battles along the front often changed from week or month to month, it was becoming necessary to support a German assault quickly when it occurred. Thus von Richthofen's four units could move as a whole even if they had to be distributed on different local airfields, but still close to each other. It was not envisaged that all four *Jastas* would fly together, as it would be too large a formation to handle for one leader, but they would often fly in two-*Jasta* groups, or even more, but pretty much independently of the others. These formations should not be confused with *Jagdgruppen*, which came later and were temporary groupings of a few *Jastas*, formed for support of specific actions and then disbanded, or regrouped with other units.

Actions in the air had been rather fewer than they had been during April and early May, the Allied airmen taking a breather from the intense actions during the Arras battle. Towards the end of June, *JGI* received its charter from HQ to form, and it was desired that the unit be able to maintain air supremacy over whatever front-line sector became involved in offensive or defensive operations. In the initial stages it was required to be based around the Courtrai area (still on the Fourth Army front), so von Richthofen took over the château at Marcke, where *Jasta 11* would fly from, while *Jasta 4* would be at nearby Cuene, *Jasta 6* at Bissenghem and *Jasta 10* at Heule.

Allmenröder might well have taken over command of *Jasta 11*, but he was killed in action on 27 June with his new *Jasta*. Another loss had been Brauneck, killed on the 26th, having scored nine victories. Therefore Wolff took over *Jasta 11*. *Jasta 4* was commanded by *Oberleutnant* Kurt von Döring, and he would also be deputy commander of *JGI* in Manfred's absence. *Jasta 6* was led by *Oberleutnant* Eduard Ritter von Dostler, and *Jasta 10* by *Leutnant* Albert Dossenbach. However, the latter was killed on 3 July, his place being taken by *Oberleutnant* Ernst Freiherr von Althaus.

Meanwhile, Manfred had shot down four more Allied aircraft in the second half of June, bringing his score to fifty-six. Number fifty-four came on 23 June, but historians were never able to identify the victim. When researching the Baron's list of claims, I tried desperately to find a British Spad fighter that might have been in action with German fighters on the evening of the 23rd, but initially failed to do so.

There being only two Spad squadrons in France narrowed the search to 19 and 23 Squadrons. The action had taken place, according to von

Richthofen, north of Ypres at 2130 hours, German time, which would have been around 2030 British time. No. 19 Squadron was based at Lietters; its operational area, therefore, was too far south of Ypres. The other was 23 Squadron, based at la Lovie, almost due west of Ypres, which made the odds far better.

However, there were no combat reports surviving in the squadron's file of such documents, nor was there any report of casualties, either in Spad fighters or pilots. The chances of it being a French Spad, while not totally impossible, the location was far too north - on the British front - to be so. Nor were there any French casualties anywhere near von Richthofen's evening action.

Following several attempts at trying to locate any reference at all to 23 Squadron having been involved, I finally got lucky by trawling through No. 22 Wing's records and found a copy of a Combat Report on file, dated 23 June. It had been dictated to the squadron recording officer by Second Lieutenant D. P. Collis of 23 Squadron, referring to a three-man offensive patrol led by himself, along with Second Lieutenants R. W. Farquhar and D. A. A. Shepperson, flying Spads B1531, B1530 and B1696. The action that occurred was timed at 2015 hours, north-east of Ypres.

Baron von Richthofen's report read:

I attacked, together with several of my gentlemen, an enemy one-seater squadron on the enemy's side. During the fight I fired at a Spad some 300 shots from shortest distance. My adversary did not start to curve and did nothing to evade my fire. At first the plane began to smoke, then fell, turning and turning to the ground, two kilometres north of Ypres, without having been caught.

While this translation might be suspect it suggests that the Spad had not made any attempt at turning until finally it began to spin down. The

Rittmeister did not say he had seen it crash, merely that it was going down without the pilot (in his view) making any attempt at pulling out. In his report, Collis stated:

> While on Offensive Patrol I sighted a formation of about six machines just N.E. of YPRES. I attacked with 2/Lts Shepperson and Farquhar. 2/Lt Farquhar singled out a machine and closed right up to within 20 yards, firing at it, but he was at once attacked from behind. I drove off his attacker and then attacked a second, but was promptly attacked myself by three E.A.[Enemy Aircraft] 2/Lt Shepperson attacked these and a general melée ensued, during which I saw a machine falling in flames, completely out of control. 2/Lt Farquhar's petrol tank and radiator were shot through and he had to make for the lines and leave the fight. I was closely pursued by three E.A. while 2/Lt Shepperson was engaging four E.A., which he continued to do until joined by some Sopwith Scouts, when the E.A. cleared off East.

This is clearly the report of the action with *Jasta 11*, and the 'smoke' seen by von Richthofen was the vaporising petrol and escaping steam from Farquhar's damaged engine and radiator. It seems probable, too, that the 'flamer' seen by Collis was also Farquhar's Spad. The proof that Farquhar not only survived but got home is that he was again flying Spad B1530 the next morning on another patrol, the mechanics obviously repairing whatever damage had occurred. Robert Farquhar, from Dulwich, south London, survived his encounter with the Red Baron, but was killed in action at the end of October 1918, flying with 32 Squadron.

* * *

Victory number fifty-seven came on 2 July, and no doubt everyone thought this was the start of another run of victories by their leader. However, that was not to be.

On 6 July a morning patrol of FE.2s from No. 20 Squadron flew to cover the area Comines-Warneton-Frelinghein, between Ypres and Armentières. In command was twenty-five-year old Captain D. C. Cunnell, with Second Lieutenant A. E. Woodbridge in the front observer's cockpit. The FEs carried some 20lb bombs while they were patrolling and dropped them on a supply dump at Houthem. Soon after turning back they were engaged by a large number of German fighters. Members of the patrol estimated the number to be about thirty.

A large air battle developed, the FEs going into a defensive circle which edged slowly towards the trenches. In this way each observer could help protect the tail of the FE ahead of him, knowing another observer was protecting his aircraft from astern. The fight lasted quite a time and the German fighters knew the dangers of opposing this British defensive tactic, but they tried nipping in when a gap appeared likely.

In reality the German fighters would dive in, fire and quickly wing-over and go down, before pulling up to make another approach. For their part, the British crews, blazing away at them, could easily believe a burst of Lewis gun fire had hit home and the opponent was falling. Several Albatros Scouts were seen to go down in this way; indeed, Cunnell and Woodbridge thought they had hit at least four. Cunnell's machine, as leader, carried streamers to indicate this, so might well have received more attention than his companions, and the crew later reported that one of the enemy machines that began to dive away was red. It therefore became a part of history that this crew had done the damage.

What damage? Richthofen was hit, a bullet creasing his skull, exposing the bone, while ripping a hole in his leather flying helmet. He was immediately blinded, probably due to a shock to his optic nerve, and was unable to move his arms. As his Albatros went down, it must have been terrifying for the Baron, being unable to see or reach for the controls, and not able to fully understand what was happening. However, moments later he regained his sight and his temporary paralysis disappeared. He quickly regained control, spotted a field in which to put down, pulled out of the dive and landed intact.

On the ground not far away was a German observation post, manned on this day by *Leutnant* Hans Schröder. After the war he wrote a book, *An Airman Remembers.* A former soldier and airman observer, he was used to seeing air battles over this sector and knew how to recognise friend and foe. He could recognise the Richthofen aircraft because of their red colouring, and on this day he was watching as they engaged in what he described as the famous 'merry go round' squadron. He also saw a red aeroplane hurtle down vertically but, about 200 metres from the ground, it levelled out, heading in his general direction. About one kilometre away it landed, saw the occupant climb out, stagger and fall to the ground.

Schröder and a corporal, the latter carrying bandages, ran to the spot, finding Richthofen lying with blood trickling from a head wound. His eyes were closed and he was as white as a sheet. With the help of his corporal he managed to bandage the injury, then Schröder sent his companion off to get an ambulance. Several soldiers had turned up by this time and, shortly afterwards, the ambulance arrived. Schröder accompanied the Baron to Menin hospital, but Manfred refused to be helped, insisting that he be taken back to Marcke. The doctor turned away with an air of resignation and the two officers were quickly on their way to the château. Here the *Geschwader* doctor administered to him, shaving off the hair around the wound while the chief surgeon probed the wound under anaesthetic. It had been a close thing.

Donald Cunnell, from Norwich, would never know that he and Woodbridge had probably downed the famed Red Baron, for he was killed six days later. On a patrol with another observer, a piece of shrapnel from an anti-aircraft shell exploding nearby, killed him, his observer just about managing to get the FE home and down. Woodbridge survived the war, later became a pilot, and served in the RAF post-war prior to his own premature death.

Richthofen never appeared to be the same man following his close encounter with death. He felt he had made a mistake by closing into a dangerous situation and paid the penalty. He made few major mistakes during his encounters in the air. He would only make one more – on 21 April 1918.

* * *

The very nature of these whirling dogfights is that, with no end of bullets criss-crossing the sky, one can never be certain of where any end up, or even if they hit an intended target. On 6 July 20 Squadron's pilots and gunners reported 'shooting down' eleven German Albatros Scouts. Squadron records show that Cunnell and Woodbridge accounted for at least one, while Lieutenant C. R. Richards and his gunner, Lieutenant A. E. Wear, claimed another.

When he was researching the life of von Richthofen, Floyd Gibbons met Woodbridge in London and talked about the von Richthofen fight, Gibbons merely working on articles for *Liberty* magazine at the time. Following publication of the articles, Woodbridge became inundated with correspondence about the air battle, and had to write to Gibbons about it. This was November 1927, at which time he was serving with No. 58 Squadron, RAF, at RAF Worthy Down, having become a pilot. Woodbridge wrote:

Dear Gibbons,

No doubt you will recall our meeting in London last Christmas when we discussed the late war and such kindred subjects, in connection with some articles you were writing of Richthofen's life.

I, naturally, thought nothing more about it, especially as at that time you were doubtful as to whether *Liberty* would publish. Imagine my surprise when recently I received a whole bunch of letters from complete strangers in America, asking for more details of my show with Richthofen.

Now all this is very nice and large, but if I remember at the time of our interview, we didn't quite decide whether it was actually I who fired the shot which wounded the German ace. The fact that he was wounded in that particular scrap on the day in July 1917, is, I think, correct, but what proof have you that it was my machine?

As Cunnell was the leader with streamers, his machine might have been more conspicuous but then the deputy leader also had streamers [although] arranged in a different manner. Did Richthofen mention anything of this nature in his book?

You see there must have been more than one Hun shot down out of control in that fight and I fail to see why I should be given the credit unless you have some confirmation from the other side. I wouldn't trouble you, but with all this publicity, one likes to be sure of one's ground.

Floyd Gibbons had been a war correspondent for the *Chicago Tribune* and had been in France in 1918 with US forces. He lost his left eye whilst attempting to rescue a wounded American soldier, receiving the *Croix de Guerre avec Palme*. He died of a heart attack in September 1939, aged fifty-two.

In Gibbons' subsequent book, *The Red Knight of Germany* (1930), he must have satisfied Woodbridge about the encounter for he quoted his words as two Albatros Scouts attacked head on:

Two of them came at us head-on, and I think the first one was Richthofen. I recall there wasn't a thing on that machine that wasn't red, and, Gosh, how he could fly! I opened fire with the front Lewis, and so did Cunnell with the side gun. Cunnell held the FE to her course, and so did the pilot of the all-red scout.

Thank God my Lewis didn't jam. I kept a steady stream of lead pouring into the nose of that machine. He was firing also. I could see my tracers splashing along the barrels of his Spandaus and I knew the pilot was sitting right behind them. His lead came whistling past my head and ripping holes in the bath-tub [front gondola of the FE].

Then something happened. We could hardly have been twenty yards apart when the Albatros pointed her nose down suddenly and passed under us. Cunnell banked and turned. We saw the all-red plane slip into a spin. It turned over and over and round and round. It was no manoeuvre. He was completely out of control. His motor was going full on, so I figured I had at least wounded him. As his head was the only part of him that wasn't protected from my fire by his motor, I thought that was where he was hit.

Although this reads more like language from an American journalist than a serving RAF officer, no doubt this is the gist of the interview the two men had towards the end of 1926. Possibly Gibbons' paraphrasing was influenced by the need to ensure the reader could understand how the Baron was shot down. By the time the book was published, however, Albert Woodbridge was dead. While flying a de Havilland Hercules G-EMBZ of Imperial Airways, he was killed in a crash at Jask Aerodrome in Persia in September 1929.

Manfred and Lothar von Richthofen. Between them they would be credited with 120 victories and both are seen here wearing the coveted Blue Max at their throats.

The Baron's all-red Albatros D.III. When not operating over a battle zone, his machines would have a white rudder and wheel covers, as well as a white nose spinner. The Albatros Company logo can be seen on the top of the rudder. This picture, at some stage, has been crudely doctored to show the national marking, edged in white, on the fuselage.

Manfred speaking to General Ernst von Hoeppner, General Officer Commanding the German Air Service, with *Oberst* Hermann von der Lieth-Thomsen, on the left. The latter was Chief of the General Staff to the Commanding General of the Air Service. (May 1917)

Manfred with his father. Manfred held
the rank of *Rittmeister* – cavalry captain.
A son could not outrank a father if he
was also on active service, so Manfred
was never able to be promoted further
while his father was still on the active list.

Manfred in his leathers, ready for flight.
Not the most flattering picture, he looks
a bit like the 'Jaws' character in the James
Bond movies.

Karl Schäfer in his Albatros D.III Scout (D1724/16). Note the flare cartridges just in front of the cockpit, and the rear-view mirror attached to the centre section of the top wing. He fell in combat on 5 June 1917, whilst *Staffelführer* of *Jasta 28*.

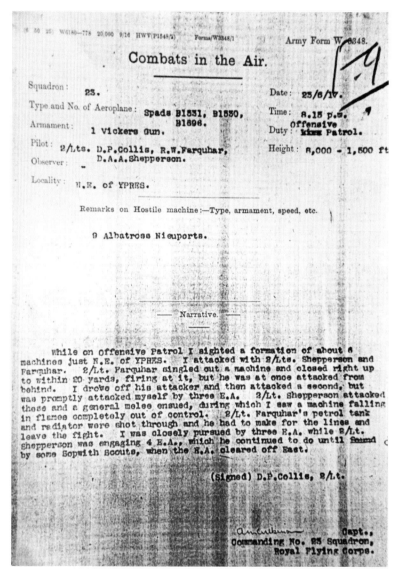

One of the mysteries of Manfred's eighty claims had been scored on the evening of 23 June 1917. North-east of Ypres he had attacked and claimed a Spad fighter but there was no obvious Allied loss. There was an outside chance that it was a French machine, but neither 19 nor 23 Squadrons had lost anyone. Quite by chance I located a combat report in Wing records, referring to a fight in which Second Lieutenant R. W. Farquhar of 23 Squadron had been hit in combat and his petrol tank and radiator had been holed, leaving a trail of white 'smoke' as he headed down for a landing. It was this vaporised steam and petrol that caused the Baron to claim an opponent down in flames. This is the combat report of the action.

Farquhar later flew with 32 Squadron in 1918 but was shot down and killed in combat on 30 October, just twelve days before the Armistice. In this line-up of 32's pilots, Farquhar is second from the right, with his legs crossed. Lieutenant A. A. Callender, 4th from the left, was also killed in this fight – against Manfred's old *Jasta 2*. Both men were minor aces, Callender being an American with the RAF, Bob Farquhar coming from south London.

Manfred's Albatros D.V in which he made a successful forced landing on 6 July 1917. Note that only the tail, nose and wheel covers appear to be painted red. The dark area by the cockpit is the shadow from the top wing. Hit by a single bullet from a Lewis gun from a FE.2d of No. 20 Squadron, he suffered a wound to the top of his skull that temporarily blinded and paralysed him. Only at the last minute did he recover sufficiently to effect this force landing in a field near Wervicq.

A rearwards view of Manfred's Albatros, serial number 4693/17.

Richthofen's Albatros being salvaged from the field. Already the top wing has been removed together with the wing V-struts and the aircraft's two machine guns.

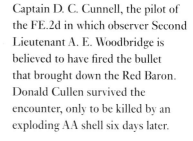

Captain D. C. Cunnell, the pilot of the FE.2d in which observer Second Lieutenant A. E. Woodbridge is believed to have fired the bullet that brought down the Red Baron. Donald Cullen survived the encounter, only to be killed by an exploding AA shell six days later.

Second Lieutenant Albert Edward Woodbridge, the observer flying in a 20 Squadron FE.2d, believed to have fired the fatal bullet that cut a deep groove in the Red Baron's skull.

The field near Wervicq, alongside a road, where von Richthofen effected a successful forced landing after being wounded in the head on 6 July 1917. This picture was taken by the author during a visit to the area in April 2006.

A good view of the FE.2d machine, showing how effective it could be with the pilot having one fixed Lewis gun to fire forward, while the observer had two Lewis guns, one moveable to cover a 180-degree arc of fire in the front, with the second gun, on a pole. If attacked from the rear, the observer, could, by unclipping his safety belt, stand on his seat, turn towards the rear and operate the gun, firing it back over the top wing. Note, too, the bomb racks beneath the lower wings, and the camera fixed to the side of the observer's cockpit. The observer was a multi-tasker if ever there was one. The crew in this picture is Captain F. D. Stevens and Lieutenant W. C. Cambray MC, an ace crew in 20 Squadron. Bill Cambray sent me this, and several other photographs during correspondence, when he was living in Australia.

Left: Manfred with his head bandaged after his wound on 6 July. He did not return to his command until the 26th and did not score again until 16 August.

Below: His injury remained bandaged for many weeks. This picture was taken following the award of the *Pour le Mérite* to Eduard von Dostler, on 6 August 1917 after he had downed his twentieth enemy aircraft. He flew with *JGI*'s *Jasta 6*, having earlier flown with *Jasta 13* and *Jasta 34b*. On this occasion, Manfred placed his own Blue Max about von Dostler's neck. Over the next several days von Dostler brought his score to twenty-six but was killed in combat with a British RE.8 on the 21st. Being a Bavarian, von Dostler became eligible for the posthumous award of the Bavarian Military Max-Joseph Order, thereby becoming a Knight (*Ritter*).

Chapter Five

Summer 1917

Summer 1917 saw the fortunes of the German fighter force on the Western Front confronted by a number of new Allied fighters. The pushers, except for the FE.2d machines, had all gone, replaced by the British SE.5 and Sopwith Camel fighters. The Sopwith Pup was being phased out, while the Royal Naval Air Service was operating with their Sopwith Triplane fighters. The French had Nieuport Scouts and Spad VIIs, with the new Spad XIIIs starting to arrive.

The Allies continued to take the air war to the German side of the lines and while the German fighter pilots still achieved a fair measure of combat success their improved opponents were not so easily overcome as they had been in the first half of 1917.

British two-seaters were still the old BE variants and the RE.8; and the Sopwith 1½ Strutters struggled on. The Bristol F2.b squadrons were getting to grips with their improved versatile tactics when faced with serious opposition, and so were fast becoming dangerous to do battle with.

* * *

JGI was based around Courtrai (Kortrijk), Manfred having returned to the château next to the airfield on Montigny Farm, on 26 July. It was just a few minutes walk from the château, through the gates and onto the airfield. To visit the other *Jastas* would take only a short drive.

It is true to say that von Richthofen was not the man he had been following his serious wounding. It is as if he suddenly realised his mortality, knowing that his skill and past experience would not always protect him. He remained at the head of *JGI* for the whole of August and into September, but only scored four more victories. His fifty-eighth came on 16 August, the fifty-ninth ten days later, followed by his sixtieth and sixty-first on 2 and 3 September; these were all he achieved.

The first was over a Nieuport 17 of 29 Squadron, then a Spad VII of 19 Squadron, an RE.8 from 6 Squadron and finally a Sopwith Pup of 46 Squadron on 3 September. Only one was a reconnaissance machine, the other three scouts, so while no doubt more careful than hitherto, he was still able to outfight three single seaters. The Pup on 3 September was of interest as Manfred, some of his pilots, and the aircraft designer, Anthony Fokker, on a visit, were able to drive to the scene and meet the luckless British pilot. The other factor was that he had just started flying the new Fokker Dr.1 Triplane (102/17, Werke Number 1729). It had been delivered on 21 August.

Anthony Fokker had come up with this new design following the perceived success of the British Sopwith Triplane which the Royal Naval Air Service had been using during the summer. It had several good qualities, including a wonderfully fast turn, thanks to the rotating le Rhône engine and the wing loading of three wings. Fokker had arranged for the first examples to be flown to Courtrai in August and these had been assigned to Manfred and Kurt Wolff, their serial numbers being Nr.102/17 to *Jasta 11*, and 103/17 to *Jasta 10*. At this stage, of course, they had not been overpainted in red, being just factory green/grey dope-streaked finish, with a natural aluminium cowling and pale turquoise undersurface.

According to his own combat report of 1 September, Manfred thought the lack of awareness from the British crew was due to the two men thinking they were being approached by a Sopwith Triplane, Manfred seeing the observer stand upright without making a move for his gun. Manfred's fire wounded the pilot, Lieutenant J. B. C. Madge, and killed the observer, Second Lieutenant W. Kimber. Kimber had only been with his squadron a few days and no doubt his final thoughts were 'why are we being attacked by a "friend"?'

When, on the next day he downed the Pup, Manfred noted in his combat report that the Fokker Triplane was 'absolutely superior to the British Sopwith'. He was also moved to write that in his view the British pilot – Lieutenant A. F. Bird – was a very skilful pilot. He remarked that when hit and forced down to some fifty metres from the ground, he did not give up, for he fired on a column of German troops while he was flattening out for a forced landing. Even then, he deliberately ran his crippled Pup into a tree to cause sufficient damage so that it would be useless to the enemy.

Algernon Bird, from Norfolk, landed near Bousbecque, to the south-west of Courtrai, and Manfred quickly drove to the scene while Bird was still there. Several photographs were taken of the Pup and of Bird, smiling for the camera, no doubt feeling extremely lucky to be alive, especially having been shot down by the Red Baron himself.

The arrival of the Fokker Dr.I was a departure from biplane fighters, and the first flight in 103/17 had been made by the mercurial Werner Voss of *Jasta 10* on 29 August. Manfred made his first flight in 102/17 on 1 September. Further examples of the Fokker Triplane began to be ferried in once Manfred, Voss and Wolff all gave their approval to the new design. It took a while for *JGI* to acquire a full complement of Fokkers and so the more junior pilots and newcomers had to continue to fly Abatros Scouts and Pfalz D.IIIs.

Mention of Werner Voss cannot pass without comment. This twenty-year old from Krefeld had been in the hussars prior to moving to aviation and had gone through the two-seater route, in his case

KG4, but in November 1916 he requested fighters, and so was posted to *Jasta 2*, where he first met Manfred. Between 27 November and 9 May 1917 he shot down twenty-eight Allied aircraft and received the Blue Max. Later in May he moved to *Jasta 5*, shooting down a further six British machines. He then had a period as acting commander of *Jasta 29* until 3 July, at which time he became acting commander of *Jasta 14*, but only until the end of that month, when he moved to *Jasta 10*. Prior to this last move, Voss had been away on leave, in June, going with Manfred to visit the latter's home. Whilst in Germany Voss had been able to test fly the new Triplane at Fokker's factory at Schwerin, the machine known then as the Fokker V5. He liked the new machine very much.

On 10 August he shot down a French Spad for his thirty-fifth victory, and his first since 6 June. Three more in August were followed by ten more in September, bringing his score to forty-eight. The forty-eighth was downed at 0930 on the 23rd, and that afternoon his two soldier brothers arrived to collect him for the start of home leave for them all. However, with fifty kills so tantalisingly close, he did just as Manfred had done at the end of April, and attempted to secure a few more victories that afternoon. Taking off alone, in his yellow-nosed, yellow-tailed Triplane 103/17, he was determined to get two more victories so that he could return to Germany and family with his score at fifty.

The scrap he got into is well documented and has become known as perhaps the greatest air fight of the war. After a skirmish with SE.5s of 60 Squadron, he was engaged by a flight of 56 Squadron's SE.5As and, although he had the opportunities to break off combat and fly home, he continued, putting bullets into practically all the British fighters, although he was unable to get a definite result. Finally he succumbed to British gunfire, crashed and died. *Jasta 10* was taken over a few days later by *Leutnant* Hans Klein from *Jasta 4*.

His loss was the second blow to Manfred and to *JGI* during this month. Just over a week previously, Kurt Wolff had fallen in combat with a Naval pilot of 10 Naval Squadron in 102/17 on 15 September. The Naval pilot, Norman MacGregor, was flying a Sopwith Camel, 10 Naval having re-equipped from Triplanes in the summer. Wolff had achieved thirty-three victories, all flying the Albatros Scout. Manfred, on leave since 6 September, was greatly saddened by both these losses, but continued his leave till 24 October. Even upon his return he did not score another victory until almost a month later, number sixty-two falling on 23 November, a DH.5 of 64 Squadron during the Battle of Cambrai.

Victory number sixty-three came on 30 November, an SE.5A scout from 41 Squadron. He and brother Lothar, together with *Leutnant* Seigfried Gussmann, engaged ten British machines that afternoon, Manfred's victory falling in flames. Gussmann shot down another.

This was effectively von Richthofen's last action for 1917. There was no other fighter pilot even close to his sixty-three victories. Voss had been getting close but he had fallen. Manfred was again sent off on leave from 12 December, although he was back for Christmas, and then on 28 December went to Russia where he remained until the end of January 1918.

From time to time, *Jasta* leaders would be summoned to conferences to discuss the changing circumstances at the front. This particular gathering was at the *Jastaschule* at Famars. Richthofen is sixth from the left in his fur coat. A number of well-known faces can be picked out and in particular the officer at the back in the light-coloured cap, 7th from the right. This is Karl Bolle, commanding *Jasta 2* Boelcke. Josef Mai of *Jasta 5* stands in the doorway, left hand side.

Something to smile about. Kurt Wolff, Constantin Krefft, and Manfred in his leather flying jacket.

Manfred von Richthofen landing one of his all-red Albatros Scouts.

Wreckage of a Nieuport 17C Scout, thought to be Manfred's fifty-eighth victory, scored on 16 August 1917. Second Lieutenant W. H. T. Williams of 29 Squadron did not survive, dying six days later in a German hospital.

An Albatros D.V (2059/17) flown by von Richthofen and seen here in the *Zeughaus* (armoury) in Berlin after the war. The Baron claimed his fifty-eighth and fifty-ninth victories in this machine. It was destroyed in the bombing of the city during the Second World War.

Manfred's opinion of many of Germany's First World War aeroplanes was sought. In this picture he is seated in a Roland D.III at the LFG Roland Works in the summer of 1917. Apparently he was not impressed.

Manfred with his Danish wolfhound, Moritz. He had purchased him earlier in the war from a Belgian civilian. After Manfred's death, Moritz was looked after by *Leutnant* Alfred Gerstenberg, a *Jasta 11* pilot, and eventually taken back home to Germany where he lived on a farm for many years.

Moritz was not the only dog with *JGI*. Manfred and Lothar watch another dog and its master.

Richthofen, in leather coat and helmet, on the airfield, with his Albatros D.V. Note that only the nose and tail are red.

In late August 1917, the new Fokker Dr.I Triplane was brought to the front by its designer, Dutchman Anthony Fokker. This picture shows a group of high-ranking German officers visiting *JGI* at Markebecke at this time. To the left of von Richthofen is *Oberleutnant* Fritz von Falkenhayn (son of General Erich von Falkenhayn, Chief of the German General Staff), who had been a member of *BAO*. Almost centre in the light coat is the German Chancellor, Dr Georg Michaelis. The bearded man is General Friedrich Sixt von Arnim, commander of the German Fourth Army.

Krefft, Anthony Fokker, Wolff and von Richthofen as the new Fokker Dr.Is started to arrive.

Manfred talking to Werner Voss. Voss had been with *Jasta 2* at the end of 1916, just prior to Manfred being assigned to command *Jasta 11*.

Manfred and Fokker seated in a car
prior to a test flight in the new Fokker
Triplane fighter.

Anthony Fokker in the cockpit of 102/17, explaining things to Major General Fritz von
Lossberg, Chief of the General Staff of the German Fourth Army. Manfred is next to the
General while on the extreme right is *Leutnant* Hans Adam, *Staffelführer* of *Jasta* 6.

Hans Adam was a Bavarian, a married man with two children. After service as a two-seater observer in 1916 he became a pilot and, following a period with *Jasta 34b*, moved to *Jasta 6*. He took command of this unit at the end of August 1917 and received the Knight's Cross of the Military Max-Joseph Order, becoming *Ritter* von Adam. He was killed in combat on 15 November.

Voss, on the right, talking to the Austrian Crown Prince Otto von Habsburg (centre), in front of Fokker 103/17, September 1917.

A smiling Voss seated in his Albatros Scout.

Voss taxiing out in his Triplane. It had a chrome-yellow cowling with white eyes around the air cooling inlets, white moustache, and a yellow rudder. He was shot down in this aircraft on 23 September in a fight with 56 Squadron.

Above: The last photograph of Werner Voss, taken on the afternoon of 23 September. His soldier brothers, Max and Otto, had arrived to journey with him back to Germany. However, Werner decided to fly one more sortie in an attempt to bring his score to a round fifty.

The Richthofen brothers in front of a Fokker Dr.I.

The Sopwith Pup B1795 marked Z flown by Lieutenant A. G. Bird of 46 Squadron on 3 September 1917, who was captured. As he force-landed, Bird ran his fighter into a tree, crumpling the starboard wings and smashing the undercarriage.

Richthofen with Algy Bird following the latter's capture on 3 September 1917. Two soldiers are in the centre. Bird was the Baron's sixty-first victory.

Manfred and *Leutnant* Eberhardt Mohnicke of *Jasta 11*, standing near Bird's crashed Pup. Mohnicke scored nine victories in the First World War.

Kurt Wolff, leader of *Jasta 10*. He had scored thirty-three victories and been awarded the Blue Max but fell in combat with Sopwith Camels of 10 Naval Squadron on 15 September 1917, flying in one of the new Fokker Triplanes.

Boelcke and von Richthofen were not the
only ones to collect souvenirs from downed
opponents. Here Kurt Wolff sits in his room with
some pinned to the wall, together with a portrait
of Manfred on the table. The number top left,
7691, was taken from an 11 Squadron FE.2,
shot down on 31 March 1917. A3338, above the
Baron's picture, comes from the BF2b of 48
Squadron he downed on 11 April.

Following the loss of Wolff, *Leutnant* Hans Klein of *Jasta 4* was posted to command
Jasta 11. Seen here on the right, Klein claimed twenty-two victories before losing his
right thumb in a dogfight on 19 February 1918. He had been awarded the *Pour le Mérite*
on 2 December 1917. Klein served in the *Luftwaffe* in the Second World War.

Chapter Six

The Final Months

Having left the Western Front at the end of December 1917 for Russia, Manfred was away for the whole of January 1918. Both he and Lothar had been invited to Brest-Litovsk by Prinz Leopold of Bavaria, Commander in Chief of German forces in the east. The war with Russia was at an end and the Richthofen brothers had been asked to attend, along with other well-known people, a peace conference with the Russian revolutionary government under Vladimir Lenin. It proved a useless attempt by the Germans to impress the Russian delegates.

During the visit the boys visited the former Czar's palatial hunting lodge for some hunting. However, with little progress being achieved with the Russians, Manfred was brought back to Germany on something of a goodwill tour, staying in Berlin for a number of days, visiting factories and meeting workers. He also went to Aldersdorf airfield where he inspected and test flew a number of new designs, including the prototype of the Fokker D.VII, which impressed him. At the end of the month he made his last visit to the family home at Schweidnitz, in Silesia. It was also the last time he would see his mother.

By this time, with the threat of American might arriving in France, and with war in Russia over, the German High Command wanted to make a big push on the Western Front. Manfred knew the plans, and in mid-March the day of the attack drew near. Meantime, Manfred had not increased his score, and probably did not do a great deal of flying until the middle of March 1918. Then, on the 13th, brother Lothar was badly injured in a fight with BF.2bs of 62 Squadron, whose gunfire shredded the Triplane's top wing. He would be out of action until July. His score stood at twenty-nine.

Although Manfred and the Fokker Triplane appear synonymous, Manfred only secured his final eighteen victories with one, the other sixty-two all being on either Albatros or Halberstadt scouts. However, *JGI* was now mostly equipped with the Triplane, although some difficulties were starting to appear, upper wing failures being a serious one. Manfred, having flown the new Fokker D.VII biplane in Germany, became anxious for its arrival in France.

On 12 and 13 March Manfred downed two more British aeroplanes, a Bristol Fighter and a Sopwith Camel. Another Camel went down under his guns on the 18th.

The big German offensive, Operation MICHAEL, began on the 21st and came as a bit of a surprise to the British front-line soldiers and the Germans made massive gains in ground, pushing their front line deeper into Allied territory. From now until his death, Manfred would be heavily engaged leading his *JGI* in an attempt to secure some kind of air superiority over the battle front, which was being heavily contested by the British squadrons, not only in aerial battles but by the use of ground-attack sorties, bombing and strafing German troops. Manfred was now flying an all-red Dr.I so that anything he shot down over the front, in no man's land, could be seen by front-line observers.

Manfred scored again on the 24th, an SE.5A of No. 41 Squadron, followed by a Camel of No. 3 Squadron the next day; he would meet 3 Squadron again. This was followed by another SE.5A on the 26th, from 1 Squadron in the early evening and, an hour later, he downed an RE.8 in flames. The next morning, he engaged in a fight with Camels of 73 Squadron, shooting down an experienced fighter pilot and minor ace, Captain T. S. Sharpe, who was in line to be awarded a decoration. Although he became a prisoner, Sharpe did receive the DFC, but it came several months after his being shot down, so it was a Royal Air Force decoration, as the RNAS and the RFC had merged on 1 April 1918, to become the RAF. Until then the equivalent RNAS decoration would have been the Distinguished Service Cross, while the RFC decoration was the Military Cross.

On the afternoon of the 27th Manfred got his second of the day, an Armstrong Whitworth FK.8, known as the 'Big Ack'. It was a two-seater ground-support machine and in fact, when engaged by Manfred, the crew were indeed 'molesting' German ground units. The day was not over, Manfred shooting down a third RAF aircraft soon after the Big Ack. This was a Sopwith Dolphin of 79 Squadron, a type he had not seen before, and the best description he could come up with was that it was a Bristol Fighter, with its rear cockpit covered over; he spotted that it had a double bank of inter-plane struts, just like the Bristol. The Dolphin fell in flames and broke up before it hit the ground. The twenty-four-year old pilot was an American, George Harding. In 1919 his actress sister was in France with a company entertaining troops and was determined to find his grave. After a long search she discovered a small graveyard near to where he went down and managed to persuade officials of the Imperial War Graves Commission to disinter the remains in a grave recorded as being that of an unknown airman. Despite the fact that a year had passed, she was able to identify her brother's remains and he received a proper burial at Dive Copse British Cemetery.

These victories brought Manfred's score to seventy-three, with another the following day – yet another Big-Ack – making it seventy-four. His next victories would be against the new RAF, although it is doubtful he knew about that change of nomenclature. Back in Germany, Manfred's mother had received a telegram following her eldest son's latest achievements:

28 March, evening.

Today your son Manfred shot down his 71st, 72nd, and 73rd opponents. The captain's 71st victory rounds the victory total of both your sons to 100. In thankful admiration, the Air Service and myself send best wishes to the parents of the brothers who are so proud in their achievements and so humble in their characters. In many thousands of German hearts today glow the sincerest wishes for your brave sons.

Yours faithfully,
Von Hoeppner, Commander-General of the Air Service.

On 2 April Manfred shot down an RE.8, followed on the 6th by a Camel, this one flown by another experienced fighter pilot, Captain S. P. Smith, whose machine exploded into flames and hit the ground. Smith had five victories and had been awarded the French *Croix de Guerre*.

JGI had remained around the Courtrai area till mid-November 1917 but then moved south to the Second Army Front near Cambrai. On 20 March 1918 it moved close to Awoingt, just south-east of Cambrai, but then moved again to Léchelle, on the Somme, on the 26th as the ground battle moved forward. It would remain here till it moved to Cappy, south-east of Bray, south of the Somme river, on 12 April. *Jastas 6, 10* and *11* had all been at Léchelle, while *Jasta 4* was at Harbonniéres.

On the 7th Manfred shot down two Camels, again from 73 Squadron, although he thought one had been a Spad. Ronald Adams was one of them. This is another case which early historians found difficult to identify, due to von Richthofen referring to his victim as being a Spad. The Baron had been in action with Spads before, so just why he misidentified this one is unclear. There were no longer any RAF Spad squadrons operating in France and the action took place on the British rather than the French part of the front.

Many years ago, long before I took any interest in First World War flying, I had read two novels by the film and stage actor, Ronald Adams, whose professional name was Ronald Adam. These were *Readiness at Dawn,* (1941) and *We Rendezvous at Ten* (1942). I discovered that he lived in Surbiton, in Surrey, and, living not many miles from that location, decided one Saturday morning to drive to Surbiton in the hope that I could get him to sign my copies of the two books. When I arrived there was no answer to the doorbell, and I was just about to get back into my car when he and his wife came walking along the street.

I have to say he was a real gentleman, and invited me in for tea and a chat, probably thinking that anyone carrying copies of his two books couldn't be all bad. After some time, flying in the First World War cropped up and he mentioned that he had been shot down in April 1918, by the Red Baron. I did know a little about von Richthofen but assumed that, like many airmen of the First World War, he believed he had been shot down by him.

However, he described the action in which he was surprised from behind while attacking a couple of German fighters and being wounded as well as having his Camel badly shot about. He became unconscious and the next thing he remembered was lying on the ground covered in some sort of tarpaulin. Some nearby German soldiers were talking, and Adams began to realise that they thought he was dead, so decided to make a moaning noise to attract their attention. They did and, seeing that he was not a corpse any longer, got him collected by a truck and sent off to an aid station.

When researching von Richthofen's victories I remembered my chat with Ronald Adam, the retired actor, and his real *persona*, Lieutenant Ronald Adams RAF. Cross-checking all the information, I realised that he had been correct. He had, in the meantime, become an extremely well-known and popular actor, seen in scores of films, although in minor roles, often playing senior RAF officers, such as Air Vice Marshal

Trafford Leigh Mallory in the Douglas Bader film, *Reach for the Sky*. After being shot down, Adams survived a long period in hospital and returned home at the end of the war.

I did, of course, have his signature on my two books, their storylines concerning the period in the Second World War, when he was a fighter controller at RAF Hornchurch, Essex during the Battle of Britain and later. He died in March 1979.

* * *

On the evening of the 20th Manfred with six of his pilots from *Jasta 11* attacked Camels of 3 Squadron. Manfred shot down its CO, although he was not leading the patrol and one other. They were Major R. Raymond-Barker MC, who died, the other, Second Lieutenant D. G. Lewis, who was captured. Both Camels fell in flames but Lewis fortunately survived. Lewis had seen the red Triplane curve in behind him and its bullets had set his gravity fuel tank alight. It will be remembered that Stefan Kirmaier had shot down Raymond-Barker's brother back in the early *Jasta 2* days.

Manfred had now doubled Boelcke's score of forty. Back home, his mother was fast becoming anxious about her son, and was trying to get someone in authority to make Manfred quit the front. Lothar had been badly injured and she did not want Manfred hurt either. There is no doubt Manfred was very tired, but he was scoring regularly again, and he must have thought a total of one hundred kills would be far better than eighty before retiring. The following day he would chase what he hoped would be number eighty-one.

Manfred von Richthofen landing in a Fokker Dr.I. Note white cowling, rudder and wheel covers.

Above: Lothar von Richthofen seated on the fuselage of his Fokker Triplane.

Right: Lothar was badly injured after crash landing on 13 March 1918, having sustained damage to his top wing during a fight with Bristol Fighters of No. 62 Squadron. The crew who did the damage were Captain G. F. Hughes MC (right) and his observer, Lieutenant Hugh Claye. Geoffrey Hughes was an Australian, from Sydney, NSW.

Manfred and *Jasta 10* pilots at Awoingt in March 1918. L to R: Paul Auer, Julius Bender, Alois Heldmann, Justas Grassmann, Erich Löwenhardt, Karl Bodenschatz (*JGI* adjutant), Max Kühn, von Richthofen, Hugo Schäfer (adjutant), Fritz Friedrichs, Joachim Kortüm.

A similar gathering: Erich Löwenhardt, Karl Bodenschatz, Max Kühn, Manfred, Julius Bender, Hugo Schäfer, Joachim Kortüm, Justas Grassmann.

Manfred's quarters at Léchelle. Not quite as salubrious as a château, but comfortable. Note that his hound Moritz is sitting on the wall in front of the building. No doubt the corrugated feature in the foreground is the entrance to a bomb shelter.

Kurt Wolff visiting Markebecke château in September 1917. He had been wounded in the left hand on 11 July in a fight with Sopwith Triplanes of 10 Naval Squadron. The picture was taken on the front steps and Wolff is in conversation with Constantin Krefft.

Manfred's mechanic helps to strap him into his Fokker prior to take off. Note the snowy ground and the streaked camouflage.

Another nice picture of Manfred in his leather flight jacket, helmet and goggles. When he was fatally wounded, he tore off these goggles and threw them overboard, a sign that he was badly wounded and needed cold air on his face. His belt also became a soldier's souvenir after his death.

Captain T. S. Sharpe DFC of 73 Squadron. Manfred shot him down on 27 March 1918 and he was taken prisoner.

Captain S. P. Smith of 46 Squadron. Another minor ace downed by the Baron, this being on 6 April 1918. Unlike Tom Sharpe, Sydney Smith did not survive the experience. After the war his father tried to locate where his son had been buried but his search proved fruitless and his name remains on the Arras Memorial to the Missing for flying personnel.

Looking over the twin Spandau machine guns of the Fokker Dr.I Triplane fighter.

Fokker DrI in the *Zeughaus* Museum in Berlin post-First World War. Believed to have been 152/17 in which Manfred shot down victory number sixty-four on 12 March 1918, number sixty-five on the 13th, and number sixty-six on the 18th, but returned to Fokker's Schwerin Works on the 18th for wing modifications. It was destroyed during the Second World War bombing of Berlin.

Lieutenant Ronald Adams who became von Richthofen's seventy-eighth victory on 7 April 1918. After serving in the Middlesex Regiment, he transferred to the RFC to become an observer with No. 18 Squadron. Later he trained to be a pilot and saw service flying night defensive sorties on Home Defence with 44 Squadron. He eventually got to France where he joined 73 Squadron, flying Sopwith Camels.

Ronald Adam in the role of Air Vice Marshal Trafford Leigh Mallory in *Reach for the Sky*, a face that many will recall in films during the 1940s and 1950s.

Captain Richard Raymond-Barker
MC, commanding officer of
No. 3 Squadron RAF. Part of a
patrol which was attacked by von
Richthofen on 20 April 1918, he
was shot down and killed. His
body was never found and he is
listed on the Arras Memorial to
the Missing. He was twenty-four
years of age.

Second Lieutenant David G.
Lewis, also of 3 Squadron.
Moments after his CO went down
in flames, his Camel was disabled
by von Richthofen's next burst.
His aircraft was also set ablaze
but he managed to crash land
and survive to become a prisoner.
From Rhodesia, he returned home
where he died in August 1978,
aged seventy-nine. He was the
Baron's eightieth and final combat
victory.

Right: Oberleutnant Wilhelm Reinhard of *Jasta 11*. Wounded on 4 September 1917, he returned to fly with *Jasta 6* in 1918. Upon the death of the Baron, he was given command of *JGI*. His score at that time was twelve which he increased to twenty by mid-June. On 3 July he was killed whilst testing a new aeroplane type at Aldersdorf, Berlin. Hermann Göring became the next leader.

Below: This picture of Manfred and some of his pilots awaiting the signal to take off is reputed to have been taken on the morning of 21 April 1918. L to R: Edgar Scholtz, Walther Karjus, Hans Joachim Wolff, Lische (admin officer), Manfred, Werner Steinhäuser, Hans Weiss, unknown. Note that the pilots have parachute harnesses, German fighter pilots having been issued with them, although it was not obligatory to wear them.

Chapter Seven

The Last Day

Manfred von Richthofen had lots to think about on the morning of 21 April 1918. He was probably aware that his mother was hoping to have him transferred home before his luck ran out. Brother Lothar always seemed to be in trouble, and even now was in hospital following his shooting down in March. Manfred would have been more than happy to have doubled Oswald Boelcke's forty kills, and it seems fairly certain that the magic number of a hundred victories might just be a matter of time away. Since 12 March he had shot down sixteen British aeroplanes, so, at this rate, a hundred might easily be achieved before the end of May. One hundred would be a good place to stop.

Operation MICHAEL, having achieved much, had ultimately failed. It had been followed by a series of fresh offensives, each with a different codename, in a vain attempt to regain the strategic initiative, and there was yet another push being planned along the Amiens front. With his *JGI* based at or around the village of Cappy, approximately twenty-six kilometres east from Amiens, it did not take long to be over the somewhat fluid front line across the Somme canal. The group had moved there on 12 April, the officers being housed in the nearby château, just a short distance from the village itself. There were several airfields in close proximity, all just a short drive from the château, although it is thought that von Richthofen also used a hut on the airfield just across from the château.

Since Royal Air Force fighters were interdicting German reconnaissance machines trying to observe behind the Allied lines, a day or so earlier von Richthofen had been ordered to clear the opposition. If successful this would enable the two-seater reconnaissance aircraft to locate Allied gun batteries just beyond a piece of high ground known as the Morlancourt Ridge, close to Corbie. This ridge looked down on the Somme canal and river. German forces were beginning to concentrate around the small town of le Hamel, within enemy artillery range and it was necessary to locate and destroy these British batteries before the build-up of German assault troops could continue in readiness for an attack scheduled for the 24th. These were the batteries of the Australian 53rd and 55th Field Artillery Brigades, located on the far side of the ridge and therefore out of sight of German battery gunfire.

Forward Observation Posts for the batteries were on the slope of the ridge, looking south and east, ready to report any movement by telephone along the areas in front of them. There was no great trench system here, merely a number of strongpoints built into the ridge, plus a number of machine-gun positions covering the southern slope with a good field of fire towards the small villages of Vaux sur Somme and Sailly le Sec, both situated on the northern side of the Somme canal. A main feature atop the ridge was a brickworks, its tall chimney dominating the skyline. In front of it was a large sugar-beet field across the road in front of the works, which wound from Corbie towards Bray.

The British, of course, were well aware of the need to keep German observation machines away and that, morning, 209 Squadron, equipped with Sopwith Camels, put up patrols at 0540 hours and later at 0820. At between 0935 and 0945, 209 sent out a full squadron effort of fifteen Camels in three flights of five. The first was led by Canadian Captain A. R. Brown DSC, the second by an American, Captain O. C. Leboutillier, the third by Captain O. W. Redgate. Among the fifteen were several experienced pilots and at least one fairly new boy, Lieutenant W. R. May, in Brown's flight.

At around 1020 Oliver LeBoutillier saw a German two-seater which one of his men shot down. Brown saw this action a short distance away, but then he spotted German scouts. These were aircraft of *JGI*. Richthofen had several of his *Jasta 11* with him, plus some aircraft from *Jasta 5*. They had already had a skirmish with two Australian RE.8s of No. 3 Squadron (Australian Flying Corps) following which von Richthofen found he was having trouble with one of his machine guns. After this action von Richthofen reformed one *Kette* of fighters, the pilots being himself, *Oberleutnant* Walther Karjus, *Vizfeldwebel* Edgar Scholtz, *Leutnant* Joachim Wolff and Manfred's newly-joined cousin, *Leutnant* Wolfram von Richthofen. A second *Kette* nearby was being led by *Leutnant* Richard Wenzl. Both Wilfrid May and Wolfram had been told to stay well clear if a battle started, and to head for home, often easier said than done.

As the two sides engaged and a dogfight began, pilots started selecting opponents to do battle with. As it developed, May had a shot at one Fokker Triplane but then decided it was getting too serious and began to disengage and head west as he had been instructed. Manfred saw the Camel break off, and, finding himself in a position to engage, headed down after the fleeing Camel, its pilot starting to lose height. It was at this time that Manfred's second gun began to give him problems, so that as well as trying to close and get into a firing position with the Camel, he had to release his seat belt in order to lean forward to pull back the intermittently working gun's cocking handle. His other problem was the wind. For most of the war (and even today), wind generally came from the west or south-west, blowing into German-held territory. This often aided German fighter pilots as it meant retreating Allied aircraft, perhaps low on fuel and/or ammunition, had to fight the wind which slowed their retreat. However, on this day, the wind was coming from the east, which aided any Allied pilot trying to head west, and blew a German airman towards Allied territory faster than he might be aware of. This, added to the fact that von Richthofen was, to a degree, unfamiliar with this particular section of the front, meant that he was going to be confused with the various similar bends and twists of the Somme river, and one small village would quickly be mistaken, especially flying at low level as he was now, for another.

Nevertheless, the German ace, oblivious to all this, and no doubt cursing his guns, became fixated on his target, which he must surely have thought was going to be his eighty-first kill. May had dropped to zero feet, actually keeping just above the water of the Somme. At least once his wheels actually touched the surface. Twisting his way west, if he didn't feel any hits on his Camel, he would surely have heard gunfire behind him, even if intermittent. Suddenly, ahead of him, he could see a church steeple, this being in the village of Vaux sur Somme. He would also be able to see, up ahead, the rising ground around a main bend of the river below Corbie; high ground was now becoming more prominent to his right.

Meantime, the experienced Roy Brown had seen May's predicament, and went to his aid. May had attended the same school as Brown, although they were not in the same year. Brown disengaged from the main fight and headed down in pursuit of the Triplane. Even if he had noted that the fighter was red in colour, he would not necessarily have known that it was being flown by the Red Baron. His dive was fast, but not as fast as post-war pulp-fiction writers would suggest. However, as Vaux sur Somme was approached, he saw May pull off to the right, and begin to head up the gradient of the Morlancourt ridge. Richthofen was caught out by the manoeuvre, having been forced to concentrate on low flying as well as his gun problems. The two fighters had skimmed along the Somme canal, May's wheels actually touching the water on two occasions and he almost got the German to fly into the church steeple. However, Manfred too turned to the right, still following the fleeing Camel.

Brown's speed and position made it impossible, without risking wrenching off his wings, to make a vigorous turn after the Fokker, but he did open fire in the desperate hope that his gunfire might at least deflect the German pilot's attention long enough for May to gain some distance. To a degree it worked, although Brown was forced to break to the left, but he was determined to bank round to the right when safe to do so and continue up the ridge as well, at the far side of Vaux, with Corbie off to his left. Doing this, he passed close to Sergeant Gavin Derbyshire's pontoon bridge location (see below).

May roared up and over the ridge and, dropping down the other side, headed roughly north, in the general direction of 209's base at Bertangles. Richthofen also headed over the ridge and could not have failed to see ahead of him, certainly at this low height, the Australian guns, even if they were covered with camouflage netting. These guns were those being sought by the German field commanders. One has to wonder what went through his mind at that moment.

With the batteries were two Australian gunners, who helped with cooking, and whose other task was to man defensive Lewis-gun positions should the batteries be attacked from the air. The Forward Observation Post had already telephoned the batteries, informing them that a British and a German aircraft were heading in their direction, and the two men, Gunners Robert Buie and William Evans, had raced to their guns. Within moments, they could see the two aircraft heading over the ridge towards them, the Camel being pursued by a Triplane. With the two men was another Australian, Private Frank Wormold, who watched the scene unfold as his two companions waited to fire. Neither gunner could open up yet, as the Camel was in the way, coming straight towards them, but no sooner did it flash by than they did fire. The radial-engined Triplane was still low to the ground and no sooner had the gunners started to fire than the Triplane pulled round to the right, heading back towards the crest of the ridge. Buie felt certain he had hit the fighter, but moments later it was out of sight as it crested the ridge.

On the far side of the beet field, across from the brickworks, and where the ridge sloped down towards the Somme, were several Australian machine-gun positions. As the Camel and Triplane had initially headed along the canal from the east, few gunners had been ready, or expecting, to fire. Sergeant Cedric Popkin headed one team and, although he grabbed a gun and began to fire as the Triplane whooshed past and below his position, it had all happened so quickly he had failed to register a hit. Once the aircraft had headed by and up and over the ridge, with Corbie off to their left and passing close to a quarry near the top of the ridge, Popkin deduced that there was a good chance that the Triplane might well turn, reappear over the ridge and have to gain a little height to get over an elevated bucket conveyor, taking material from a quarry across the Bray road northwards.

Popkin was ready and, if as one might suppose, the Baron lifted the Triplane slightly to scale the conveyor, it would have given Popkin a better view of it. Even so, it needed his already proven skill as a gunner to have the courage to fire well ahead of the moving target, so his bullets would hit it. Popkin opened fire.

All this time, behind him, down on the canal, Sergeant Gavin Derbyshire, who had been supervising a party of soldiers during the repair of pontoon bridges, had, moments before, witnessed two and then a third aircraft, heading towards Vaux from the east. As he watched he saw the leading machine nip past the church tower, hurriedly followed by the second, which he identified as a German Triplane. He later said that he was only aware of a third aircraft a short while later, but it was not in direct contact with the first two. As he continued to watch, he saw the first two climb over the ridge, and moments later the German one reappeared. It was also level with him as he looked north, up the ridge, and suddenly the German machine jerked upwards for a moment before plunging to the ground.

Some distance away, one of von Richthofen's pilots, *Leutnant* Joachim Wolff, had seen the chase begin and later said:

> I looked for the Rittmeister and saw him at a very low height somewhere over the Somme and not far from Corbie. He was still pursuing the Camel. I shook my head and wondered why the Rittmeister was following a machine so far behind the enemy lines.

As soon as the cry went up that a German machine had been brought down a short distance in front of the brickworks, any number of soldiers, mostly Australian, headed for it. In a nearby trench, Gunner Ernest Twycross of the Royal Garrison Artillery, on spotter duty with his officer overlooking the Somme canal area, had seen the enemy machine come down. Seeing the Triplane had force-landed rather than crashed, the officer told Twycross to run across and capture the pilot before he set light to his machine. Twycross did so, and arriving, found the German still alive but covered in blood. The pilot said something fairly indistinct, but definitely including the word 'Kaput', before he slumped forward. Twycross was becoming aware of a horde of Australian 'diggers' fast approaching, so, with nothing to take captive, he headed back to his trench.

Some of the Australians got von Richthofen's body out of his cockpit and laid him on the ground. His face was bloody and there was blood down his chin and the front of his flying jacket, and on his knees and fur overboots. Another person to arrive was Private Wormold, who had been with Buie and Evans. Looking through the throng of fellow Aussies, he noted the blood etc., and when he went back to the battery position, told his two pals that they must have got him, because the

German had been hit in the chest and, of course, Buie was convinced it was his fire that had caused the Triplane to turn right. As the story grew, he began the story that he and Wormold had seen the bullets hitting the German in the chest. Just how this was possible cannot be explained for, quite apart from the large rotary engine, cowling, machine guns and windshield, anyone on the ground would be hard put to even see the top of the pilot's head.

* * *

Of interest are the written words of both Brown and May in their flying log-books. Brown wrote of his ninety full-minute patrol:

> (1) observed 2-seater Albatros shot down in flames by Lieut Taylor.
> (2) dived on large formation of triplanes and Albatros single seaters. Two triplanes got on my tail, so I cleared off. Climbed up and got back to scrap. Dived on a pure red triplane which was on Lieut May's tail. Got in good burst when he went down. Observed to crash by Lieut Mellersh and Lieut May. Dived on two more triplanes which were chasing Lieut Mellersh. Did [not] get them. Red triplane was Baron von Richthofen, confirmed by medical examination by Australian R.E.8 squadron and 11th Australian Brigade.

Although these personal notations often get muddled, Brown's original combat report was rewritten once the identity of the German pilot became known. On the first one the name of May was added after Mellersh's, then it was re-typed so that the additional name did not look like an addition. Again, on the original, the combat was marked 'Indecisive', but nothing was written on the second report, either 'decisive' or 'indecisive'. Wilfrid May wrote in his log-book:

Engaged 15 to 20 triplanes – claimed one. Blue one. Several on my tail came out with red triplane on my tail which followed me down to the ground and over the line on my tail all the time, got several bursts into me but didn't hit me. When we got across the lines he was shot down by Capt. Brown. I saw him crash into side of hill. Came back with Capt. We afterwards found out that the triplane (red) was the famous German airman Baron von Richthofen. He was killed.

Overlooking the grammar and punctuation, May's words seem to confirm what he had experienced but, one suspects, amended slightly once the facts became known. It was only May's third war patrol, his first two having been flown the previous day. During the very first one his flight became involved in a scrap with some Fokker triplanes.

May's combat report for the 21st, timed at 1045, mentioned his attack on a Triplane with 'blue camouflaged wings', and read:

Attacked large formation of about 15-20 machines. Engaged one E.A. firing bursts head on into engine, he went over and dived down. I was unable to observe result as a second machine attacked me from behind. I fired at a second machine without result. I then went down and was attacked by a Red Triplane which chased me over the lines low to the ground. While he was on my tail, Captain Brown attacked and shot it down. I observed it crash into the ground.

It is difficult, logically, to see how May would have seen it 'crash to the ground', or see it 'crash into side of hill'. It seems more likely he was coached by the squadron's Recording Officer so as to ensure Brown got the credit. Two other reports, one by Lieutenant Mackenzie and one by Mellersh, are included here. Mackenzie's opponent he described as having a brown fuselage with blue spots on its wings:

One Triplane came on to me from left side firing and hit me in the back, the bullet just grazing me. I then did a steep left hand bank and he did a right hand turn. I then gave him a good burst from behind and at about his own level. He turned over on his back and seemed to hang there. I did not see him afterwards as I was compelled to leave owing to pain from wound.

The combat was marked 'Indecisive'. Mellersh's report:

I followed Captain Brown down onto a large formation of Fokker Triplanes and Albatros D.Vs. A dogfight ensued and I managed to get on the tail of a Triplane with a blue tail. I fired about fifty rounds into him when he turned and I got a long burst into him when he was turned up. The Triplane then dropped his nose and went down in a vertical dive. I followed, still firing, and saw machine crash near Cerisy. Two other Triplanes then dived onto me and I was forced to spin down to the ground and return to our lines at about fifty feet. Whilst so returning, a bright red Triplane crashed quite close to me and in
looking up I saw Captain Brown.

This report was marked 'Decisive'. It also appears to be typed out to make it certain that Brown was responsible. I should also record that Brown's actual report noted that the fights was against a *Fokker Triplane, pure red wings with small black crosses*:

(1)   At 10.25 a.m. I observed 2 Albatros burst into flames and crash.
(2)   Dived on large formation of 15-20 Albatros Scouts D.5 and Fokker Triplanes, two of which got on my tail and I came out.
    Went back again and dived on pure red triplane which was firing on Lieut May. I got a long burst into him and he went

down vertical and was observed to crash by Lieut Mellersh.
and Lieut May.

I fired at two more but did not get them.

This report was marked 'decisive', but appears to have had 'In' added later to make it 'Indecisive'. Perhaps one should note that he did not see the Triplane crash himself, and the Triplane going down 'vertical' suggests it was at some height, not as low as it actually was. One needs to note the full stop after Mellersh, because the 'and Lieut May.' was typed in later, necessitating the typing of a second combat report so that this add-on was not obvious.

Typed on the amended report was:

Engagement with red triplane:
Time, about 11-00 a.m.
Locality, Vaux sur Somme.

* * *

Eventually, aware that the scene was in full view of German observers across the river, and with a strong possibility that the downed aircraft and the troops milling around it might be shelled, everyone was dispersed. Shells might usually be expected to be fired, but a German observer in a church tower at Hamelet had seen the action and would not have ordered guns to fire in case the German pilot was still alive.

Eventually the Baron's body was taken to 3 Squadron AFC's airfield at Poulainville, being placed in a hangar, together with what remained of the Triplane after the Australian souvenir hunters had finished with it; there it was souvenired some more.

That evening von Richthofen's body was cleaned up, photographed, and made ready for inspection by some army doctors who would make a cursory post mortem. As a result it was obvious that the Red Baron had been hit by a single bullet, which had struck him on his right side, passed through his body and exited just below his left nipple. The doctors made the examination with a piece of fence wire, concluding that the bullet had probably ripped through the aorta at the rear of the heart, which caused the gush of blood through the mouth and down the front of the Baron's coat, whilst also splashing onto his knees and boots. This explains why soldiers had been saying the Baron had been hit in the chest and upper legs. Other so-called witnesses, reported seeing bullet holes in his face, back, front and stomach, none of which occurred. Some facial damage had occurred due to Manfred hitting the gun butts because his harness was still undone.

On 23 April 1918 what seems to be an official press release appeared in newspapers, although a number of 'facts' are incorrect, including 'The German champion crashed, *smashing his machine to smithereens*' whilst also stating 'Only one bullet [hole] was found in his body, and that had gone straight through the heart, *entering on the left side*'.

A later, seemingly official, report – marked SECRET – reported the following, apparently based on evidence of eyewitnesses, written down immediately after the event. It states that the Triplane was heading straight for the defensive guns of the Australian positions. I shall quote just a few lines from it:

Richthofen was firing into the plane [May] before him but it was difficult for the Lewis gunners to shoot owing to the British plane being directly in the line of fire. They accordingly waited their time until the British plane had passed. Richthofen's plane was not more than 100 yards from each when they opened fire. The plane was coming frontally towards them so that they were able to open fire directly on to the person of the aviator. Almost immediately the plane turned N.E. being still under fire from the Lewis guns. It was now staggering as though out of control. Further effective bursts were fired: the plane veered to the North and crashed on the plateau near the brickworks.

The aviator was already dead. There were *bullet wounds in the knees, abdomen, and chest. The plane was badly smashed ....*

Once more reported 'facts' are wide of the mark and appear to report hearsay evidence. Had the author of it known about the single bullet wound entering from the aviator's *right* side, the report would have been very different. One might also wonder if the press release, mentioned earlier, had changed the entry point of the bullet wound to help the claim that the Buie and Evens fire must have hit the Baron after he had turned to the right, thereby exposing his left side.

* * *

When preparing von Richthofen's body for inspection, an orderly, taking off clothing, discovered a bullet as it dropped to the floor, which had been in the left-hand fold of the flying jacket. The Baron's only other clothing is recorded as being red silk pyjamas. This was witnessed by other orderlies present but the finder just popped the bullet into his pocket and it was not spoken of again. It was later taken home to Australia and remained in a kitchen drawer for many years.

The point of this is, however, that, as the bullet had not exited the jacket, it is estimated by ballistics experts that it had been fired from around 600 yards. Any closer it would have gone right through body and coat and out the side of the cockpit. Study of Popkin's location and the crash site shows the distance to be approximately 600 yards. This, in addition to Sergeant Derbyshire's recording exactly the spot

Manfred's Triplane jerked upwards, like someone digging him in the ribs, thereby causing him to pull back on the stick, adds to the final scenario. Lastly, although one will never really know for certain who fired the fatal shot, Popkin was certainly experienced in how to lead a moving target. He was 600 yards away, and was the only person known to have fired a bullet that would have hit the Baron on the German's right side. Popkin was later to say:

> As (von Richthofen) came towards me, I opened fire a second time and observed at once my fire took effect. The machine swerved, attempted to bank and make for the ground, and immediately crashed.

* * *

On 24 April a German newspaper carried a report by Herr W. Scheuermann, its special war correspondent on the Western Front, headlined 'Richthofen's Last Flight'.

> Last Sunday morning Richthofen with four other machines of his *staffel*, set out to attack enemy aircraft. Two of the aeroplanes of Richthofen's flight were manned by experienced fighter pilots, *Leutnant* [H.J.] Wolff and *Vizfeldwebel* [E.] Scholtz. The other two machines were flown by *Leutnant* Karjus, who after the severe wound sustained in 1914 which resulted in the loss of his right hand, was for many years a brilliant observer and has lately joined the fighter squadron, and *Leutnant* [Wolfram] von Richthofen, a young cousin of the *Rittmeister*.
>
>   In the neighbourhood of Hamel, *Leutnant* Wolff and *Leutnant* Karjus became involved in a fight with seven British Sopwith Camels. Another flight of seven Sopwith Camels came to the assistance of the first, while at the same time a German flight of Albatros aeroplanes, flying at the time over Sailly-le-Sec, rushed

up. Part of the British flight escaped the Albatroses which set off in pursuit. Wolff and Karjus remained in close combat with three or four Sopwith Camels, when quite suddenly Richthofen's red machine flashed past and forced down an enemy machine in a steep nose dive.

Meanwhile, *Leutnant* Wolff shot down one of the remaining enemies in flames, this being his ninth victory. Looking down on to the crashing machine, he caught sight of Richthofen, who was still pursuing his enemy low down in a westerly direction towards the Somme. A second later *Leutnant* Wolff was engaged in single combat by a very clever enemy. After shots having been freely exchanged, the enemy who had several bullets in his machine, broke off the fight, his machine gun having apparently jammed.

Wolff was then able to look round quietly and ascertained that Richthofen's machine had disappeared in the direction of Hamelet. On the return flight he was obliged with the other German airmen to go in pursuit of a British squadron which met them. By the time they returned to their aerodrome there were already to hand a number of reports from airmen and artillery observers showing unanimously that Richthofen, against his usual practice, had followed his opponent some eight kilometres behind enemy lines. With a fresh east blowing he finally shot his enemy down, after which he had tried to climb his machine again. This manoeuvre was unsuccessful however, probably because the elevator had been hit or owing to engine trouble. The nose of the machine immediately went down again, and Richthofen had brought his machine down on enemy territory in a steady though steep dive without any damage.

It was generally assumed that the 'Siegfried of the Air' had fallen into enemy hands and was uninjured as it was thought impossible that a wounded man could have landed the heavy triplane so successfully. The news of the death of the hero, which was received with great excitement everywhere on the front and at first was not believed, first came through the wireless messages of the enemy. Since then a rumour, of which I do not know the source, has been current in this sector and is being widely spread, that Richthofen was killed after he had stepped out of his machine by the Australians, in whose divisional sector the machine had landed. The place where his glorious life ended is north of Corbie, on a flat hill near where the Ancre runs into the Somme.

Richthofen as was his practice when flying was not carrying any papers or badges and this time not even wearing the order 'Pour le Mérite', which he otherwise always wore under his fur coat. But the enemy knew his triplane, which since the beginning of the great battle he had painted red as before. The sight of which always caused jubilation in the German infantry, and in the columns, just as it filled the enemy with fear.

The hero's aged father, who is acting as a Town Mayor in Flanders, received the news with admirable composure. He has wired to the squadron which still bears Richthofen's name, stating that he hopes the spirit of his son will remain alive in his surviving comrades. The pilots, who mourn the loss of their leader, swear by the memory of the leader that they will avenge his death.

Apart from some journalistic assumptions, etc., the fact that von Richthofen was thought to have been killed whilst on the ground, was accepted for some time, but it is interesting to read about his landing. People who know the Fokker Dr.I have said before that the aeroplane was difficult to fly 'dead stick', confirming he was still able to bring it down and have the automatic good sense to cut the engine and depressurise the fuel tank.

A German artillery observer in the church tower at Hamelet had seen the machine come down. Whether he actually suspected the pilot was von Richthofen or not, he would have seen that the pilot had not left the cockpit, so would be reluctant to direct artillery gunfire at it. This no doubt saved a number of Australian soldiers death or serious injury.

The Morlancourt ridge, taken from the top of the Australian Memorial Tower at Villers Bretonneux. Corbie town is on the extreme left, and the Somme is out of sight but runs the whole length of the base of the ridge. The chimney of the brickworks is on the skyline. Although it is in a slightly different position here than where it was in 1918, the location remains the same. (1) Corbie; (2) over this ridge is where the gun batteries were located; (3) brickworks chimney; (4) Vaux sur Somme; (5) location of air battle prior to the chase west.

49.V.3
62ᵈ .J .21.2.
15.5.18-16

An aerial picture taken on 15 May 1918 shows the area to the east of the brickworks. What looks like a shell hole, bottom left, is the ruined windmill close by where the Australian gun batteries had their forward observation post. From here the observers saw the Camel and Triplane heading towards and below them along the canal, low down, and telephoned the battery commander that aircraft were fast approaching their general position.

The view from the windmill Forward Observation Post looking south-east. The canal can be seen amidst the trees to the right of centre.

A close-up from the same location. There were fewer trees in 1918 but it was along this waterway that von Richthofen pursued May at low level.

With Vaux sur Somme bottom left (1), May and von Richthofen were heading towards this village before turning right towards the Morlancourt ridge. The brickworks are shown in the centre (2). The old quarry site is to the left of these works. (3) Welcome Wood.

The view from where Sergeant Popkin and his machine-gun unit were stationed, looking down towards the south. Vaux sur Somme church is to the left (1) and the canal is just in front of the far line of trees.

The church in Vaux sur Somme. The signpost shows Corbie to be 4.5 km to the west, and Mericourt 4 km to the north. Picture taken in 1996.

Another view looking south-east from the FOP. The gradual slope of the ridge is seen and the Somme is below to the right. (1) Sailly le Sec.

The brickworks is almost centre of this picture (1) and the old quarry site is now trees (2). To the right, where the ground slopes away, is the site of the Australian gun batteries (3). Corbie would be below and to the left of this picture.

Another view of this same area, looking north, with the brickworks in the centre (3); (1) is the approximate location of the gun batteries. (2) shows the site of the old quarry; (4) the spot where the Baron came down; (5) pointing towards Popkin's position; (6) the Somme.

The Somme canal with a pontoon across it, approximately where Sergeant Gavin Derbyshire watched May and von Richthofen head up the ridge and where, only seconds later, he saw the red Triplane reappear. Although he could not see the brickworks from this low position, he did see the Triplane suddenly rear up at a spot that would have been nearing the front of it. He had also seen the second Camel (Brown), having turned left after his attempt at firing towards the Fokker, come towards him, pass by and begin to make a right hand turn to the north.

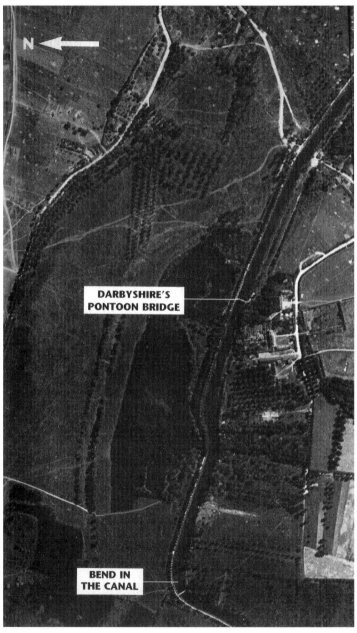

The Somme canal and a pontoon bridge stretching across it. Sergeant Derbyshire saw the three aircraft from this position, confirming that the second Camel was nowhere near the other two machines that were, by then, heading up and along the slope of the ridge. Corbie is not in view but would be beneath the bottom of this picture.

As May and von Richthofen crested the ridge, probably to the left of the quarry area, it sloped away towards a road which ran along fields where the Australian guns were located. In this picture, looking north, we can view the fields and the Corbie to Méricourt-l'Abbé road. Buie and Evans were manning machine guns in this location too, the two aeroplanes coming directly towards them.

Manfred von Richthofen was flying this Fokker Dr.I Triplane (425/17), which he had flown the previous day, downing victories 79 and 80. Note the new national markings of a straight-sided cross on wings, fuselage and tail, replacing the cross *pattée*.

Above: The same Fokker upon its arrival at Cappy, with the standard *pattée* crosses marked. They would have been overpainted before von Richthofen took it over to fly. Evidence seems to show that it was painted red at the Fokker factory, so obviously it was meant for the Baron.

Right: The serious yet handsome face of the Red Baron.

Left: Manfred being prepared for another flight over the front. Note the fur overboots, now on display in the Australian War Memorial in Canberra, still with the signs of blood stains.

Below: An aerial view of the whole area, showing the brickworks, the quarry, the line of buckets on the conveyor from the quarry, and the field where the Australian guns were situated.

NS

BRICKWORKS

The field where von Richthofen crash landed. Medical evidence confirms he would only have survived some thirty seconds before death occurred. Considering he had time to switch off his engine, decompress the fuel tank and put the Triplane into a side-slip to reduce height quickly for fear of running out of space in which to put the aircraft down, one can judge the time he had left after being hit. Having done all this, and considering the time Gunner Twycross took to get from his trench to the Fokker, it is obvious that von Richthofen must have been hit after re-crossing the crest of the ridge, with the gun batteries behind him.

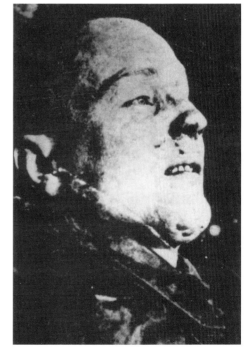

The dead Baron von Richthofen at Poulainville aerodrome on the evening of 21 April. The facial wounds were caused by hitting the gun butts as he crash landed. Having loosened his seat belt in order to lean forward to try to clear his guns, there was no restraint to hold him from doing so. The orderly who prepared the body for inspection had also to pull his front teeth forward, as they had been pushed back on impact.

The Fokker Triplane was also taken to Poulainville aerodrome, home of No. 3 Squadron AFC, where much of it was 'souvenired', although the guns, engine and seat later found homes.

German LMG 08/15 machine gun, like those used on the Fokker Dr.I.

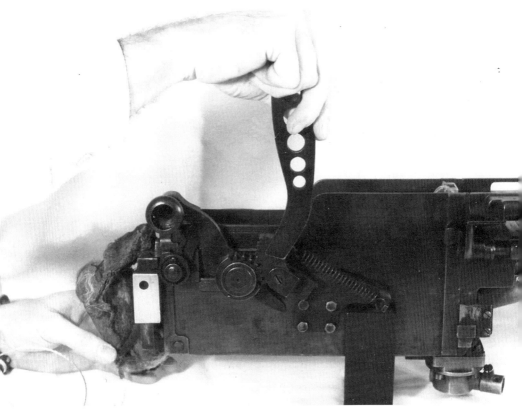

Demonstrating the crank handle in the number-3 position when trying to clear a jam. Richthofen had one gun jam while the other was misfiring due to a split firing pin. Why he did not give up and return to Cappy long before reaching Vaux sur Somme, we shall never know.

Chapter Eight

The Participants

Number 209 Squadron Royal Air Force, which had until recently been No. 9 Squadron of the Royal Naval Air Service, happened to be the Sopwith Camel squadron that encountered elements of Baron von Richthofen's *Jagdgeschwader Nr. I* (*JGI*), during the late morning of Sunday, 21 April 1918. Mostly former RNAS pilots, they had become, since the amalgamation of the RNAS and RFC on 1 April, officially members of the new Royal Air Force.

Their task on this day was to maintain air superiority over the Somme front. It was known that the Germans were preparing for an assault along this sector, and it was essential to keep the prying eyes of German airmen from flying observation and photographic sorties behind the Allied front. As far as the German airmen were concerned, *JGI* was assigned to clear any air opposition, so that these observation flights could do their job, in particular to discover the exact location of any known gun batteries somewhere to the west of the Morlancourt ridge.

Allied two-seater observation work was being carried out mid-morning by RE.8 two-seaters from No. 3 Squadron, Australian Flying Corps, and two of their aircraft were intercepted and driven off by *JGI*. It was during this skirmish that the first of von Richthofen's guns became troublesome.

Meanwhile, the Camel pilots encountered two German reconnaissance machines endeavouring to nip across the lines, shot one down, and drove the other east. Shortly after this the two fighter formations met each other and a fight developed. As a result of this action, Germany's greatest fighter pilot made uncharacteristic errors.

First he failed to realise or acknowledge that the normally west-to-east wind was blowing from east to west. Secondly, being fairly new to this sector, his knowledge of ground locations, was lacking and as a result he failed to realise that bends in the Somme with similar looking villages along it, looked very much alike, making it seem he was still farther east rather than heading into Allied territory.

His third mistake was to chase an opponent for too long, especially with poorly functioning guns, and, flying so low on this occasion, due to Lieutenant May heading down to make himself less vulnerable, he was unable to keep a careful watch on his position.

Many First World War aces were caught out by ground fire. Richthofen very rarely allowed himself to come under ground fire, just as he never attempted to attack observation kite balloons. In his view, they were far too dangerous. This day everything that could go wrong did go wrong.

The following photographs depict the more prominent participants in a battle that ended with the death of Germany's most successful fighter ace.

The British patrol of twelve Sopwith Camel F.1s was led by 209's senior flight commander, Captain A. R. Brown DSC, a Canadian from Carleton Place, Ontario. Arthur Roy Brown was an experienced pilot, aged twenty-four, and had already been credited with nine combat victories. Involved in the shooting down of von Richthofen, officialdom would credit him with his tenth victory and he would be awarded a Bar to his DSC. However, he was almost at the end of his tether by this stage and soon after the 21 April action he went into hospital at Étaples with influenza and nervous exhaustion. Roy Brown died from a heart attack in March 1944.

In Brown's flight was a new and inexperienced fellow Canadian, W. R. May from Edmonton, who had attended the same school as Brown. Following infantry service, Wilfrid 'Wop' May became a pilot and was posted to 209 in April 1918. Attacked by the Red Baron, May showed considerable skill by flying low and from side to side, although if the Baron's guns had been working properly there is no doubt he would have been shot down. Surviving this day he went on to be awarded the DFC, was credited with thirteen victories and survived the war. He died in June 1952.

Lieutenant W. J. Mackenzie was an American from Memphis, Tennessee, although raised in Port Robinson, Ontario, Canada. In the fight on 21 April he claimed to have shot down a Fokker Dr.I, although he was himself wounded, probably by *Leutnant* Hans Joachim Wolff of *Jasta 11*. Mackenzie survived the war, also flying with 213 Squadron, and won the DFC and Belgiam *Croix de Guerre*, achieving seven victories. He died in September 1959. As a Naval pilot, his 'wings' are those of a RNAS airman, whereas, in his photo, Brown has RAF wings.

London born Lieutenant F. J. W. Mellersh, was approaching his twentieth birthday and had joined the RNAS in October 1916. On joining 9 Naval his first aircraft was the Sopwith Triplane. He was to gain five victories in all, the fourth being yet another Fokker Dr.I during the fight on 21 April. He remained in the RAF, rising to become Air Vice Marshal Sir Francis Mellersh KBE AFC MA. Sadly he was killed in a helicopter accident in May 1955. In this picture he is dressed formally as a Naval officer, with the traditional winged collar.

Leading B Flight of 209 was another American, from New Jersey, Captain O. J. LeBoutillier, who joined the RNAS in Canada in 1916. With 209 he gained four victories flying the Sopwith Triplane before changing to the Camel. On 21 April 1918 he helped shoot down the two-seater encountered before the big fight commenced. He ended the war with ten victories. After the war, Oliver 'Boots' LeBoutillier remained a pilot, flying in all sorts of jobs, including stunt-flying in Hollywood films, and even gave aviatrix Amelia Earhart her first dual-instruction flight in twin-engined aircraft. He had over 19,000 flying hours and died in Las Vegas in May 1983.

Lieutenant R. M. Foster, from Surrey, England, had a successful career with the RFC in 1917, and 209 in 1918. He shared the two-seater shot down on 21 April 1918 with LeBoutillier. Ending the war as a captain, with sixteen victories and a DFC, he remained in the RAF, becoming Air Chief Marshal Sir Robert KCB CBE DFC and died in Suffolk in October 1973.

Lieutenant M. S. Taylor was also in B Flight, seen here in his 'fug' boots and Naval 'wings'. Another Canadian in 209, he came from Regina, Saskatchewan, and had joined 9 Naval Squadron in late 1917. He was credited with seven victories and received the French *Croix de Guerre*, but was shot down and killed on 7 July 1918, by the German ace Franz Büchner of *Jasta 13*. On 2 May 1918 he had shot down *Leutnant* Hans Weiss of *Jasta 11*, another participant on 21 April. Merrill Samuel Taylor was twenty-five.

Lieutenant O. W. Redgate led C Flight on 21 April. From Nottingham, Oliver Redgate joined the RNAS in 1917 and remained with 9 Naval/209 RAF until he was wounded on 15 May 1918, by which time he had achieved sixteen victories and been awarded the DFC. Sadly he died of TB in 1929.

Lieutenant C. G. Edwards came from St Albans and, following training with the RNAS, joined 9 Naval early in 1918, which then became 209 Squadron RAF. He was also in C Flight and by mid-August had shot down seven enemy aircraft and been awarded the DFC. He was killed on 27 August, his aircraft being hit by an artillery shell.

Leutnant Hans Joachim Wolff, along with *Oberleutnant* Walther Karjus engaged Francis Mellersh in the air fight, and had not Roy Brown come to his rescue he might well have been outmanoeuvred and shot down. Wolff (no relation to Kurt Wolff) from Mulhausen claimed a Camel on 21 April, one of a total of ten victories he was credited with before his death on 16 May 1918. His very first victory, on 18 March 1918, had been over Lieutenant Anthony McCudden MC, the younger brother of Major J. T. B. McCudden VC DSO MC MM.

Oberleutnant Walther Karjus had lost his right hand and forearm earlier in the war but had managed to fly once an aircraft was modified to allow him to hold the control column with his prosthetic limb. He flew with *Jasta 11* for two months. He later commanded *Jasta 75* and was killed in 1925 whilst piloting an aircraft.

Left: Leutnant Hans Weiss, from Hof on the Austrian border, was two days past his twenty-sixth birthday when he was engaged in the air battle on 21 April 1918. By this time he was a very experienced pilot, having flown two-seaters before becoming a fighter pilot with *Jasta 41* in 1917. With ten victories he was posted to *Jasta 10* in March 1918, but was then made acting commander of *Jasta 11*. On 21 April he was awarded the Royal Hohenzollern House Order, but fell in combat on 1 May, shot down by Lieutenant M. S. Taylor of 209 Squadron.

Right: Leutnant Richard Wenzl, after service with two-seaters on the Eastern Front, became a fighter pilot, first with *Jasta 31* and then *Jasta 11* in March 1918. Minutes after the 21 April fight, he was flying past Corbie and Hamelet, heading for Cappy, and noticed a small aeroplane on the ground on the ridge. Upon his return to Cappy, this information, together with Wolff's sighting of the *Rittmeister* chasing a Camel towards the same location, gave everyone cause for concern. In the Second World War he was adjutant to the German ace Werner Mölders, and survived the air crash in which Mölders was killed in November 1941. Wenzl died in February 1957.

Jasta 11's *Leutnant* Edgar
Scholtz, from Suhl,
Thuringia, had scored six
victories by April 1918,
although his commissioned
rank did not come until after
his death. That occurred on 2
May 1918, stalling his fighter
whilst taking off from Cappy.
This was the same day as
Weiss was killed.

Leutnant Wolfram von Richthofen,
Manfred's cousin, born in Barzdorf, Silesia.
He and Wilfrid May appeared to have
tangled briefly during the fight on 21 April,
but Manfred had come to his rescue, and
then began the chase after May's Camel
which ended so disastrously. Wolfram
ended the war with eight victories. He later
served in the German *Luftwaffe* during the
Spanish Civil War, and in the Second World
War, becoming a *Generalfeldmarschall* [and
commanding the Luftwaffe in Italy until
retired on medical grounds in late-1944]. He
died of a brain tumour in June 1945.

Sergeant Cedric Bassett Popkin, from Sydney, Australia, was with 24 Machine Gun Company, Australian 4th Division. He and his section were situated at the top of the slope heading up the Morlancourt ridge, so was able, once he collected his thoughts and grabbed one of the guns, to get in a quick burst or two at the red Triplane as it passed below him from left to right before climbing towards the crest of the ridge. Estimating that the enemy machine might very well re-appear over the crest but on the far side of the quarry area, he swung his gun round in anticipation of another shot and was rewarded by seeing the German aircraft indeed re-appear. It was some 600 yards from him, fairly low down and it was going to take all of his experience to aim well ahead of the target so that his bullets might find their target. He was assisted by Privates Rupert Weston and Marshall. Popkin survived the war, although he lost a leg in the closing weeks. He died in January 1968. His brother Rowland, with the Artists' Rifles, was killed in action in France, on 27 September 1918, aged twenty-four.

Gunner Ernest Wilfred Twycross, Royal Field Artillery. His location on 21 April was in a forward observation post to the right of Popkin's position with a clear view across the valley to the east. He and his officer's attention had been caught as the two aircraft flew along the Somme below them, and the firing of many guns at the second one. Once the Triplane re-appeared over the crest and was seen to be hit and crash land, his officer told Twycross to run over and take the pilot prisoner. On reaching the Triplane he saw the badly wounded and very bloody pilot, who said only a word or two before dying. This information – related by his son, following a last visit to the Western Front by the old soldier prior to his death in June 1971 – was presented to the Imperial War Museum, who forwarded its contents to me.

In the distance is the church at Hamelet, south of the Somme, from where a German observer watched the Triplane come down in the field in the foreground. As there was a chance that the pilot was still alive or wounded he did not order German artillery fire on the position. Had he done so there might well have been casualties amongst the Australian troops who swarmed the area.

The original grave of the Red Baron in Bertangles cemetery on 22 April 1918. He was buried with full military honours, the service being conducted by the Reverend Captain G. H. Marshall DSO, chaplain with No. 101 Squadron RAF.

Among many objects that were taken from the downed Fokker, was the control column. To left are two rectangular gun triggers, marked L and R. On the top is the coupé button for the magneto, while to the right is the finger grip, and on the left is the auxiliary throttle control. The small holes at the base are where the cables from the throttle and triggers pass through.

Chapter Nine

What Remains?

There has been a constant fascination surrounding the life – and death – of *Rittmeister* Manfred Albrecht *Freiherr* von Richthofen for almost a hundred years. Much has been written in books and articles, from the serious historian, to the pulp fiction writers of the immediate post-First World War years, whose lack of factual awareness caused speculation and invariably became accepted truths. Only a few years ago one historical aviation group member was wondering when enough was enough, but the Baron continues to fascinate and be read and written about.

I have been just as guilty as others in continuing to write about him, but I would like to think that the book I wrote about his victories in *Under the Guns of the Red Baron* along with the late Hal Giblin, and Nigel McCrery, put on accurate record his achievements in air combat. Certainly no one has come forward to imply we got any of our eighty conclusions wrong, and indeed we managed to clear up several mysteries.

Then I became interested in his death, especially when the collection of pre-Second World War letters sent to John Coltman produced some very interesting eyewitness accounts of 21 April 1918, most of them from men who had not been contacted by later writer/historians Pat Carisella (*Who Killed the Red Baron* in 1969) and Dale Titler (*The Day the Red Baron Died*, 1970). Sadly, John Coltman died serving in the RAF during the Second World War, but his collection of letters remained. When the late Alan Bennet and I were researching for our book *The Red Baron's Last Flight* in 1997 we had two pieces of information. One vitally important was discovered in the Coltman file, which helped to clinch 'when' von Richthofen died. It was a letter from Gavin Derbyshire, describing how he had witnessed the Triplane suddenly pull up, its pilot obviously being hit, and there was Ernest Twycross's later account to his son about reaching the downed fighter in time to see the Baron actually expire. Two eminent pathologists told us how long von Richthofen's serious wound would take to end his life, so it could then be deduced as to when the bullet struck.

While it is now impossible to discover who actually fired the fatal bullet, and nobody will, it certainly cleared many mysteries about who did *not* fire it. In January 2015 I was asked to accompany an Australian TV (Channel 9) crew to the Morlancourt ridge in France, to explain the topography of the place von Richthofen fell and where the various gunners were located. While the reporter who did the interviewing tried gallantly to make me say who actually killed the German ace, she had finally to accept that while evidence indicated Popkin, it could still have been any soldier in the vicinity who managed to get off a shot at him, provided he was located to face von Richthofen's right side.

The following pictures depict a gallery of interesting aspects of the Baron's life and flying career, together with pictures of interest taken in more modern times.

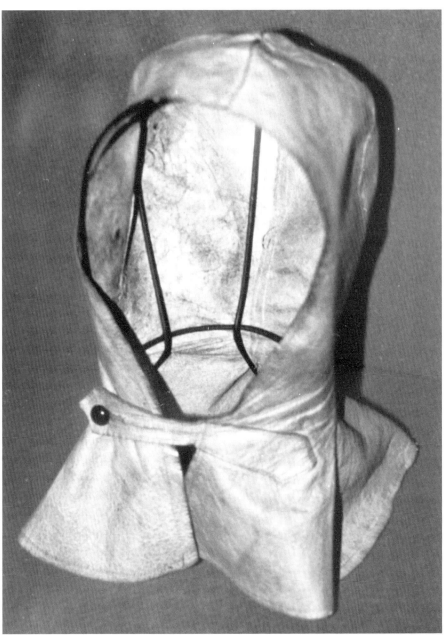

One of von Richthofen's flying helmets, presented to the RAF Museum where it is on display. Obviously it is not the one he was flying when shot down, nor the one he was wearing when wounded in July 1917. It is light brown in colour and made of soft leather and was donated to the Museum by the von Richthofen family.

Among several items taken from Manfred's body was this German one-mark bank note.

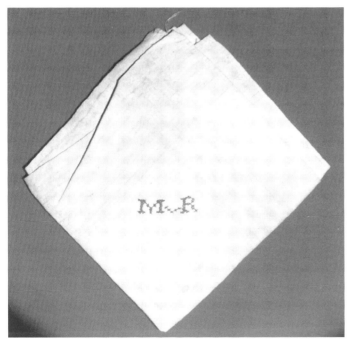

Also this white handkerchief, his initials MvR sewn in red.

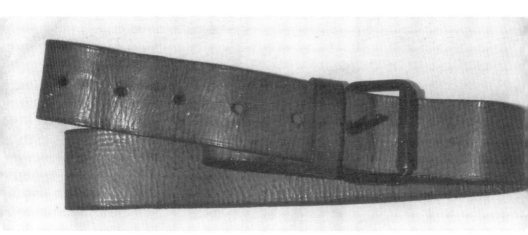

Richthofen's brown belt. It is not always appreciated that he was wearing a parachute harness on his last flight.

A modern aerial view of the field between Bertincourt and Vélu where *Jasta 2* was formed in August 1916, and where von Richthofen arrived as a founder member. It had already become an established German air base, *KIEK (Kampfeinsitzer Kommando)* Bertincourt having operated with Fokker Eindeckers here since the start of 1916. The village of Vélu is in the distance beyond the wood.

In mid-April 1917, *Jasta 11* moved to an airfield at Roucourt, near Bohain. The officers took over the château for their accommodation. This picture of Château de Roucourt was taken before the war.

The château was destroyed by fire in 1918 but rebuilt post-war although the top sections were changed. This picture was taken in 2000 during a visit by First World War aviation enthusiasts. Comparing it with the previous picture, the top windows are different and the roof smaller. Although the balustrades on the walls either side are now missing, please note the position of the left-hand gate which leads to the rear of the building.

The open gate to the rear garden area, situated to the left of the entrance of the château.

Kurt Wolff and von Richthofen stand in discussion while based at Roucourt in front of the door/gate referred to above. Note the moulding above the door as seen in the pre-war picture on page 175.

Left: Brad King of the Imperial War Museum, with Baron Bequet de Mégelle, the host and owner of the château, during a visit in 2000, standing close to the spot where the previous picture was taken in 1917.

Below: The visiting group of aviation enthusiasts sitting on the rear steps of the château in 2000. Such steps were often a feature of these buildings and an ideal spot for taking group photos of resident German airmen during the First World War.

Brad King of the Imperial War Museum, standing in the field which was the airfield at Roucourt in the First World War.

Another château, this time the one used by *JGI* officers at Markebecke near Courtrai, from July to November 1917.

The rear of the château; once again we can see the steps where a number of group photographs were taken of the pilots and officers of *JGI*.

A close-up of those steps.

The front steps to the château; similar but adorned with two lions holding crested shields.

A bandaged von Richthofen seated on the front steps of the château on 30 July 1917, following his head wound on the 6th. The trophy propeller was probably from a British FE.2. Seated on the steps are Constantin Krefft, vonR, Eberhardt Mohnicke and Erwin Böhme, his old friend from *Jasta 2*, visiting the Baron. Those identified at the rear, second from the left is Karl von Schönebeck, then Kurt Scheffer, and Wilhelm Bockelmann.

The gates to the château with the building seen through the trees.

If one stands in front of the above gates and then turns completely around, this is the view of the field used by *Jasta 4* and *Jasta 11* at Marckebecke.

A visit by General Erich von Ludendorff to Marckebecke airfield on 19 August 1917. Richthofen's red Albatros D.V (2059/17) stands ready, a ladder by the cockpit should the General wish to see into the cockpit. The château is off to the right. The small road on the left runs from the main road to the buildings of Montigny Farm, where *Jasta 4* was located.

An aerial view of Marckebecke showing the location of the château and the spot where the previous picture was taken.

An aerial shot of the modern-day location of the airfield at Avesnes le Sec, near Cambrai. *JGI* operated from this base between November 1917 and March 1918.

The last move of *JGI* while von Richthofen was its leader, was Cappy sur Somme. This is the château where once again the officers were billeted, although sometimes the Baron is believed to have slept in a hut on the airfield.

One of several fields at Cappy. From one of them, Baron von Richthofen took off on his final flight in the mid-morning of 21 April 1918.

The gates of the cemetery of Bertangles village. The burial took place just about where several of the visitors are standing. After the war his remains were moved to the German Military Cemetery at Fricourt, near Albert.

In November 1925 von Richthofen's remains were removed from Fricourt Cemetery and re-interred in the *Invalidenfriedhof* 'cemetery', Berlin on the 20th, presided over by Hermann Göring, future head of the German *Luftwaffe*.

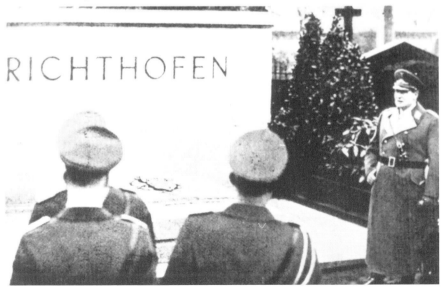

In 1996, while in Canada on a book-signing trip, I attended the *Over the Front* League of First World War Aero Historians' Seminar in Ottawa. I met Sue Fischer and Jan Hayzlett, discovering they were both von Richthofen aficionados. Determined to talk to them further I was saddened to discover they had left to visit Toronto early the following morning. Later, when I was taken to the Royal Canadian Military Institute in that city, to view the von Richthofen objects that Roy Brown had brought back with him and donated to the Institute, they were visiting there too. The display is in a sealed alcove in the restaurant, seen behind Sue and Jan in this picture. Sue was a great help, for, while visiting her then fiancé at the University of Maine, she had discovered that the Floyd Gibbons' archive was kept there. Gibbons had written *The Red Knight of Germany* in 1930 and Sue gained access to his research notes.

Today the remains of Manfred von Richthofen lie in Wiesbaden Municipal Cemetery, in a family plot, together with younger brother Bolko, who died in 1971. His sister and her husband are also here. Lothar is buried in Schweidnitz, together with their father, although a memorial plaque is here on the left. Lothar was killed in a flying accident in 1922, while their father died in 1920.

The alcove displays the aluminium seat from von Richthofen's Triplane. At one stage it was thought that the holes through the back of this were made by bullets that had, therefore, mortally wounded the Baron from the rear. The holes are in fact where screws fixed the seat to a wooden cross member. The cross was taken from the downed Fokker. A wing-tip spar is also present. Brown gave this to fellow Canadian pilot, Billy Bishop VC. Bishop's son donated it to the RCMI in 1968. Both these items, and a representative German machine gun, are set against a backdrop of a large photograph of the Baron's wrecked Fokker. The seat and cross were donated to the Royal Canadian Military Institute by Roy Brown in 1920. Although only scraps remained, the seat had obviously been covered by a red-coloured fabric; the bottom part appears to be plywood. The whole thing was riveted to a cross-member at the bottom, in similar fashion to the back. When the RCMI recorded it on the inventory they wrote 'No possible estimate of fair market value'. How true!

Quite by chance, we discovered air historian and paint expert Alan Toelle, who had been with us at the Seminar in Ottowa. He had also travelled to Toronto, having been given permission to inspect the fuselage cross from the Baron's Fokker, which had been taken out of the normally sealed alcove. Here, Alan is making a detailed inspection of the paint and varnish. He invited me to look through the magnifying apparatus, and to see the evidence of staining caused by exposure to semi-burned castor oil lubricant/fuel mixture, characteristic of that blown back from rotary engines. Overall, the red was still a bright colour but a little dirtier than the original red paint.

This is the cross Alan was inspecting. One can just make out the painted change from a *pattée* cross to the new *balkenkreuz* variety. The centre of the cross has been crudely cut away and then superimposed over a piece of canvas on which members of 209 Squadron have put their signatures. The cross was taken from the port side of the Dr.I.

A close-up of those signatures. Among them can be made out, in the left column, W. R. May, C. G. Brock, M. A. Harker, M. S. Taylor, O. C. LeBoutillier, F. J. W. Mellersh, W. J. Mackenzie, R. M. Foster, J. H. Siddall and L. F.Lomas. Names on the right include others involved in the fight: A. W. Aird, E. B. Drake, C. G. Edwards and O. W. Redgate. The only missing name is that of A. R. Brown.

Another cross, this one taken from the starboard side of von Richthofen's downed Triplane. It was later given to an American army doctor who had helped save the life of the 'new' owner. In 1994 it came up for auction in London and, prior to the sale, I visited the auction house to take pictures. I was asked if there was any way I could add confirmation that it was genuine. Looking closely at it under a magnifying glass I recognised the same discolouring of the bottom half of the cross that I had seen in Toronto. As it happened, the auction failed to reach the price required. Today it has been purchased by the film director Peter Jackson for his aviation museum in New Zealand. The piece of paper appended to one corner reads:

> This cross was taken from Baron von Richthofen's red triplane immediately after he was brought down on the morning of April 21st, 1918, near Corbie. I was there.

> 1347 L/Cpl A. C. Putnam,
> HQ Signallers,
> 22nd Battalion,
> A.I.F. France.

Manfred von Richthofen's decorations. During his career he was awarded the following: *Orden Pour le Mérite* (Prussia), Red Eagle Order, 3rd Class with Crown & Swords (Prussia), Royal Hohenzollern House Order, Knight's Cross with Swords (Prussia), Iron Cross 1st & 2nd Class (Prussia), Military Merit Order, 3rd Class with Crown & Swords (Bavaria), Military St Henry Order, Knight's Cross (Saxony), Military Merit Order, Knight (Württemberg), Saxe-Ernestine House Order, Knight 1st Class with Swords (Saxon Duchies), General Honour Decoration, 'for bravery' (Hesse), War Honour Cross for Heroic Act (Lippe), Cross for Faithful Service, 2nd Class (Schaumburg-Lippe), War Merit Cross, 2nd Class (Brunswick), Oval Silver Duke Carl Eduard Medal with Date Clasp and Swords (Saxe-Coburg-Gotha), Hanseatic Cross (Bremen), Hanseatic Cross (Hamburg), Hanseatic Cross (Lübeck), Order of the Iron Crown, 3rd Class with War Decoration (Austro-Hungarian Empire), Military Merit Cross, 3rd Class with War Decoration (Austro-Hungarian Empire), Bravery Order, 4th Class, 1st Degree (Bulgaria), Imtiaz Medal in Silver (Ottoman Empire), Liakat Medal in Silver (Ottoman Empire), War Medal (Ottoman Empire).